IMAGES OF YORKSHIRE COAL

By Peter Williams

IMAGES OF YORKSHIRE COAL

By Peter Williams

Landmark Publishing

Published by

Landmark Publishing Ltd
Ashbourne Hall, Cokayne Ave, Ashbourne, Derbyshire DE6 1EJ England
Tel: (01335) 347349 Fax: (01335) 347303
e-mail: landmark@clara.net
website: www.landmarkpublishing.co.uk

ISBN 1 84306 151 1

© **Peter Williams 2005**

British Library Cataloguing in Publication Data: a catalogue record for
this book is available from the British Library.

Photography: © English Heritage/Crown Copyright
Print: Bath Press Ltd., Bath
Design: Mark Titterton
Cover: James Allsopp

Page 2: Monckton Coke Works, Royston, Havercroft with Cold Hiendley, West Yorkshire.
Title page: Frickley Colliery, South Elmsall, Pontefract, West Yorkshire.
Front cover: No.3 Compartment Boat Hoist, Goole Docks, Aire Street, Goole, Humberside.
Back cover: Caphouse Colliery, New Road, Sitlington, West Yorkshire.

Acknowledgements

All images have come from the National Monuments Record archive. All images are either ©Crown copyright, ©English Heritage, or ©English Heritage NMR, unless otherwise stated.

Application to reproduce the images should be made to the National Monuments Record, Kemble Drive, Swindon SN2 2GZ.

The NMR negative numbers appear in square brackets at the end of the captions, with the photographer's name, where known.

The majority of the photographs were taken between 1991 and 1995 by the Royal Commission on the Historical Monuments of England photographic team based in York; Bob Skingle, Keith Buck, Roger Thomas and Tony Perry, with some printing by Keith Findlater.

Additional people-based work was also done by James O Davies, from the RCHME London office.

A number of photographs were selected from an anonymous donation made to the NMR, which is gratefully acknowledged.

Special mention must be made of the help and encouragement given by colleagues in English Heritage, particularly to Ursula Dugard-Craig, Keith Falconer and Andrew Sargent. Thanks, also, to Barry Jones, Ian Leith, Danny Parker, Ian Leonard, James O Davies and to Michael Evans for copy work and advice on railways.

The information in the photographic captions draws heavily on the research work done by Robin Thornes, Barry Jones, Sheila Ely and Robert Hook throughout the 1991-95 survey.

Thanks must also go to Lindsey Porter, at Landmark, who assisted at all stages, particularly in the selection of images.

The National Monuments Record

The National Monuments Record (NMR) is the public archive of English Heritage and provides information on the architecture and archaeology of England.

The archive has its origins in the Royal Commission on Historical Monuments (England) created in 1908 (RCHME) and the National Buildings Record (NBR) set up in 1940. The NBR joined with RCHME in 1963 and the archive was renamed the National Monuments Record. In 1999 the RCHME merged with English Heritage to form an enhanced new lead body for heritage.

The NMR collections are stored in a state-of-the-art archive, where temperature and humidity are regulated to prevent deterioration. Some ten million items relating to England's buildings and archaeological sites have been brought together under one roof where they may be consulted by interested parties.

The main parts of the collections include diverse ground photographs of England from the 1860s to the present day and 20th century air photographs from the RAF, Ordnance Survey and other bodies.

The work of individual photographers, including H.W.Taunt, Eric de Maré, H. Felton, George Watkins and Bedford Lemere is well represented.

Some of the larger collections include the Country Life magazine negatives, the measured drawings collection, sales particulars, the archives of the Survey of London, records of the Property Services Agency and records of English Heritage properties. A database can be consulted at the NMR.

Two important new on-line resources are available – 'Images of England' [www.imagesofengland.org.uk] which by 2005 will contain a photograph of each of the c370,000 'listed buildings' and 'Viewfinder' [www.english-heritage.org.uk/viewfinder] which contains selected images from the NMR.

For information on NMR services and holdings contact:
NMR Enquiry and Research Services,
English Heritage,
National Monuments Record,
Swindon SN2 2GZ
Tel 01793 414600
Fax 01793 414606
e-mail nmrinfo@english-heritage.org.uk

Preface

This book celebrates the once mighty Yorkshire coal industry as illustrated by the material held in the National Monuments Record in Swindon. It does not seek to be a history of that industry or comprehensively catalogue the material in the archive. Rather, it is a personal, and evocative, selection of images conveying the breadth and feel of material that has come together in a somewhat unsystematic fashion reflecting the increasing public awareness and interest in industrial buildings since the 1960s.

Between the late 1950s and the 1980s the English coal industry had been contracting at the rate of about 30 pits per year. At the same time the long overdue modernisation of collieries was drastically affecting the surface features. The change from steam power to electricity in both winding and ventilation was recorded by steam enthusiasts such as George Watkins and George Cooper. In 1982 two Yorkshire collieries were extensively photographed by the Royal Commission on the Historical Monuments of England (RCHME) – Caphouse and Walton.

In 1991, as a result of the predicted dramatic contraction of the industry, the RCHME embarked upon an extensive programme of colliery recording, concentrating on the 50 English pits then remaining of the c1,000, in Great Britain, that had been Nationalised in 1947. The RCHME colliery survey had three strands:

- New ground photography of the significant surface structures remaining. Some 2,700 negatives were taken of 358 sites.

- An aerial photographic survey conducted on behalf of EH in 1992. 2,000 photographs were taken of c100 collieries.

- Acquisition by copying and donation of older material including some hundreds of old photographs copied on site, c5,000 record cards and microfilm plans given by the Stavely Coal & Iron Company Ltd. Of Chesterfield [as yet uncatalogued].

This work resulted in two publications, the first, *Images of Industry – COAL*, RCHME,1994, by Robin Thornes and the second, *Colliery Landscapes*, EH, 1995, by Shane Gould and Ian Ayris. Of a total of more than 5,000 colliery project photographs taken between 1991 and 1995, only c220 have been published.

Further searching in the NMR archives at Swindon has thrown up some other coal related material pre-dating the main survey, notably in the survey material from the RCHME publication *Workers Housing in West Yorkshire1750-1920* by Lucy Caffyn and an anonymous donation of annotated photographic prints. A number of *The Illustrated London News* coal-related engravings have also been copied. With such a wealth of unused material to hand it was decided to present a selection of images of one area in detail and Yorkshire was chosen because of its seminal place within the coal industry.

If you were to say the word 'coals' you might expect to receive the reply 'to Newcastle'. If, however, you were to say the word 'miner' you will receive the reply 'Yorkshire'. This is a reflection of the importance of Yorkshire miners in the public psyche. Yorkshire miners are known for comradeship, for community, for bravery, for Yorkshire grit.

Driving through Yorkshire you might expect to see some kind of memorial to coal and miners, situated, perhaps, near the motorway at Barnsley. Something of the scale and impact of the 'Angel of the North'?

We can but dream.

Peter Williams

Images of Yorkshire Coalmining

Yorkshire has an outstanding place in the coal industry. With most of the pit structures gone and the spoil heaps flattened and landscaped there still remains a wealth of visual, historical and social evidence of coal mining throughout the country, from canals and power stations to village housing. The National Coal Mining Museum is located in Yorkshire, as is the only surviving in-situ Newcomen engine. Yorkshire can boast the first plate-rail, introduced by John Curr at the Sheffield Colliery in 1775; the first commercial use of steam locomotion at the Middleton Colliery in 1812; the first Mines Rescue Station (Tankersley); the biggest pit in Britain in the 1920s [Brodsworth]; one of the largest modern deep coal mining projects in the world (Selby) and the worst underground disaster in England at The Oaks Colliery in 1866. The Yorkshire area reports of the Children's Employment Commission of 1841 were instrumental in the banning of children under the age of ten working underground. The great shipwreck disaster in Bridlington Bay in 1871, when 30 overloaded Tyne colliers were driven ashore with 70 lives lost, led to the first Merchant Navy Act and the introduction of 'Plimsoll Lines' painted on all vessels.

The 1896 table of Yorkshire mines worked under the *Coal Mines Regulation Act* lists more than 89,000 workers above and below ground. Amongst the 345 mines, the ones with over 1,000 underground workers stand out; Acton Hall, Aldwarke Main, Denaby Main, Monk Bretton. The smallest mines also catch the eye; 'Blue Slates' owned by Squire Robertshaw of Lascelles Hall with but two workers; 'Box Ings' at Huddersfield, owned by Seth Senior and Sons, manager Eli Rhodes, with 31 workers; 'Daylight' at Batley with 15 workers; 'Breakneck' at Shibden Hall with three workers. We can but wonder at the lives and landscapes of these mysterious undertakings.

On vesting day in 1947, 123 Yorkshire collieries were nationalised. Ten more were sunk after this date. Numerous licensed mines, together with dozens of local private supply companies, employed untold numbers of mining and mining related workers. In 2005 only a handful of collieries and companies now remain of this, once, huge industry.

In geographical terms the area presented in this book encompasses Yorkshire as it was before the 1974 boundary changes. The NMR catalogues material at a county and parish level and it was felt less confusing to keep to the site addresses as catalogued at the time the records were made rather than using current postal addresses. OS grid references are supplied, where known. The material is presented alphabetically, although some sites, for example the Newcomen engine at Elsecar, have been placed within their geographical context.

The photographs reproduced are all black and white. Very little colour was taken during the main survey, firstly for archival permanence and secondly because it was felt that black and white somehow suited the subject. In some cases an image of lesser quality has been used in order to broaden the content. The drawing of the steam locomotive at the Middleton Colliery is not the most revealing image, but is the only one available and must suffice to tell the story.

The content of the NMR coal mining material is predominantly of surface buildings and structures and there is little underground material. Indeed during the 1991-95 survey the photographers were prohibited from going underground for safety reasons.

No selection of images can hope to be complete, what follows is an attempt to show the diversity of coal mining material relating to Yorkshire held in the NMR and each of us may bring to the subject their own knowledge and memories.

To some, the remaining structures and landscapes of the coal industry may be perceived as uninteresting or eyesores, lumped in with gas holders and glue factories, to be sanitised and swept away. Others may look on them with respect and pride in the monumental achievements of their forebears.

Ackroyd and Best Limited, Beacon Works, Morley, West Yorkshire.
An advertisement from *The Colliery Managers Pocket Book* 1918. Founded as Hembrigg Lamp Works, 1896-1902, the company moved to Preservence Works 1902-1911 and then to Beacon Works and subsequently became Hailwood and Ackroyd. [BB016221]

Agnes Terrace, Day Street, Barnsley, South Yorkshire. SE 344 058
Between the 13th March and the 26th March 1936, George Orwell stayed at 4, Agnes Terrace, the home of Albert Gray and during this visit he went down Wentworth and Grimethorpe Collieries. In March 1937 *The Road to Wigan Pier* was published with the essay 'Down the Mine'. The terrace is, unusually, aligned gable end to Day Street with access to the front doors from the gate at bottom right, allowing each house a small garden at the front. [AA046215 Peter Williams]

Allerton Bywater Colliery, Garforth, West Yorkshire. SE 427 277
The bridge over the railway line led from the heapstead to the spoil-heaps. In 1914 the buildings to the northwest of the winding houses comprised the sawmill, joiners shop, mechanics and smiths shops and locomotive repair shop. To the far right were the offices. A view from the northwest, photographed 12th December 1987.
[94601 Anonymous donation]

Allerton Bywater Colliery, Garforth, West Yorkshire. SE 427 277
An aerial view taken 19th October 1992, during demolition. The first shaft was sunk c1875 to a depth of 310 yards and subsequent expansion led to the exploitation of three main seams – the Haigh Moor, Flockton Thick and Silkstone. In 1954 there were 1,133 men working underground and 430 on the surface, producing 650,000 tons per year. The central feature of the photograph shows the c1980 coal preparation plant on the site of the two Baum washeries. At the lower left are the two headframes, the latticework frame is for the Silkstone pit and the other is the Flockton pit. To their right are the steam winding houses and the extended mixed pressure house.
[CCX14356/02 NBR 94601 © Crown copyright.NMR Cox Collection, NMR]

The Askern public house sign, Instoneville, South Yorkshire. SE 565 134
An exaggerated headstock dominates the Lowryesque street scene. Askern was a small spa town prior to c1890 when mining began. In 1929 Low Temperature Carbonisation Ltd began production of Coalite products. This plant ceased in 1985 and the colliery itself closed in March 1992. Photographed 24th January 1993. [AA93/01344 Bob Skingle]

Askern Main Colliery, Campsall Road, Askern, South Yorkshire. SE 565 135
The steam winding engine, a horizontal double tandem compound winder by Yates and Thom, Blackburn, 1912, No.2 Shaft is seen in excellent working order on 28th April 1979. George Watkins has 1911 as the date, see Stationary Steam Engines of Great Britain Vol.1, Yorkshire, p.78. [79/11/11 George Cooper]

Askern Main Colliery, Campsall Road, Askern, South Yorkshire. SE 565 135
Headstocks from the northwest. Under the legs can be seen an earlier lattice-work frame. Photographed 5th November 1992. [AA92/07114 Bob Skingle]

Askern Main Colliery, Campsall Road, Askern, South Yorkshire. SE 565 135
Headstocks and part of the coal washing plant seen from the south during demolition. Photographed 5th November 1992. [AA92/07119 Bob Skingle]

Bentley Colliery, The Avenue, Bentley with Arksey, South Yorkshire. SE 570 075
Sinking began c1903 and closure came 3rd December 1993. No. 1 heapstead built in 1911-12 from reinforced concrete using the Mouchel-Hennebique system. Photographed 28th April 1993. [BB93/23794 Roger Thomas]

Bentley Colliery, The Avenue, Bentley with Arksey, South Yorkshire. SE 570 075
The two cross compound steam winder from No.2 Shaft built by Fraser and Chalmers, Erith, 1908.
The winding house is roofless but some attempt has been made to cover parts of the engine. Photographed 28th April 1979. [79/11/32 George Cooper]

Bentley Colliery, The Avenue, Bentley with Arksey, South Yorkshire. SE 570 075
A general view of unknown date. [U.9 George Long]

The Memorial Fountain, Bentley Park, Bentley, South Yorkshire. SE 572 070
The sad remains of the fountain, erected in 1928 for the Miners Welfare Committee. Photographed 24th January 1993. [AA93/01049 Bob Skingle]

Brodsworth Colliery, Adwick-le-Street, Doncaster, South Yorkshire. SE 524 077
Exterior view showing the two Koepe towers built 1960-61 and the steel headgear c1935. Owned and built jointly by the Hickleton Main Colliery Company and the Staveley Coal & Iron Company, Brodsworth became the largest coal producing colliery in Britain in 1923, claiming the world record for highest daily coal tonnage. The 'biggest pit in Britain' closed 7th September 1990. [91126]

Brodsworth Colliery, Adwick-le-Street, Doncaster, South Yorkshire. SE 524 077
Cutting the first sod in 1905. The owner of Brodsworth Hall, Charles Thellusson and his wife, Constance, stand in the centre of the photograph behind the ceremonial spade and barrow. A large post of unknown purpose looms over the proceedings. The spade and barrow, which used to be on display in the Mining Room at Cusworth Hall Museum, have now been returned to Brodsworth Hall – an English Heritage property.
[A950838 by kind permission of Mr Sneap]

Bury's & Co Ltd, Regent Works, Sheffield, South Yorkshire.
An advertisement from *The Post Office Directory of Warwickshire, Kelly & Co,* 1872, showing miners' picks. [BB016222]

Cadeby Colliery, Doncaster, South Yorkshire. SE 510 001
A complex dating from 1869 with later structures, demolished in 1987. Cadeby Colliery was situated about 2,000 yards from Denaby Colliery, next to Conisborough Railway Station. Photographed 20th December 1986. [61435 Anonymous donation]

Cadeby Colliery, Doncaster, South Yorkshire. SE 510 001
Photographed 20th December 1986. [61435 Anonymous donation]

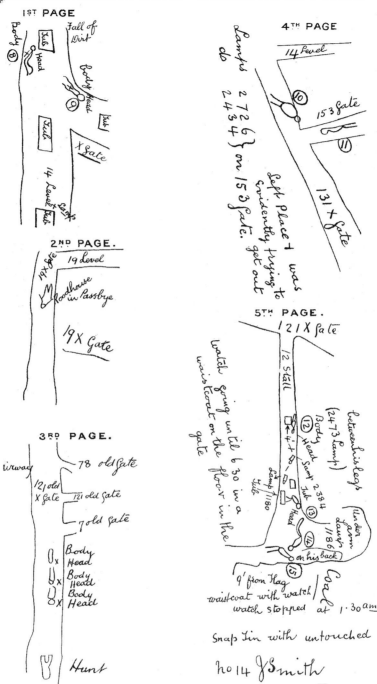

Cadeby Colliery, Doncaster, South Yorkshire. SE 510 001

On Tuesday, 9th July 1912, two violent underground explosions resulted in the loss of 88 lives. Shown here are five pages from the notebook found in the pocket of Herbert Cusworth, the Assistant Under-Manager, aged 39, who died after the second explosion. Three H.M.Inspectors of Mines were also caught by the second explosion, dying from the effects of afterdamp; William Pickering, 53, Divisional Inspector, Henry Hewitt, 46, Senior Inspector and Gilbert Tickle, 34, Junior Inspector. Figure 4 in the Home Office Report by R.A.S.Redmayne, C.B., His Majesties Chief Inspector of Mines. [BB016214]

Caphouse Colliery, New Road, Sitlington, West Yorkshire. SE 1648 2534
Dating from the early 19th century, the last coal was mined in 1985. Opening in 1988 as Yorkshire Mining Museum, the site was designated the National Coal Mining Museum for England in 1995. The following views were taken on 17th June 1981. The Steam Engine House, No.1 Shaft Heapstead, Headgear and Screens.
[BB93/08157 Peter Williams]

Caphouse Colliery, New Road, Sitlington, West Yorkshire. SE 1648 2534
Steam Engine House and No.1 Shaft Heapstead and Headgear from the northeast. [BB93/08186 Peter Williams]

Caphouse Colliery, New Road, Sitlington, West Yorkshire. SE 1648 2534
A view from the east on New Road. [BB93/08160 Peter Williams]

Caphouse Colliery, New Road, Sitlington, West Yorkshire. SE 1648 2534
No.1 Shaft base of headframe. The gates are to the upper level of the shaft entrance. [BB93/08185 Peter Williams]

Caphouse Colliery, New Road, Sitlington, West Yorkshire. SE 1648 2534
The Boiler Yard and Steam Engine House. [BB93/08173 Peter Williams]

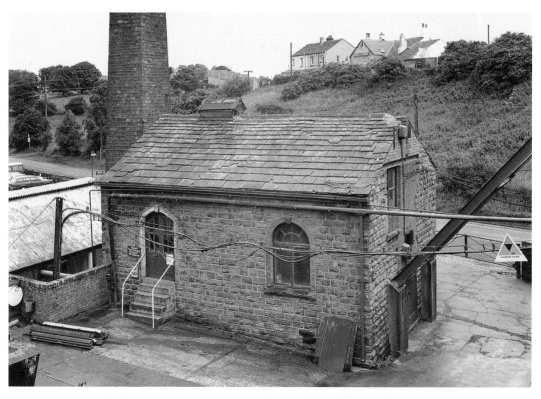

Caphouse Colliery, New Road, Sitlington, West Yorkshire. SE 1648 2534
The Steam Winding House seen from the west. [BB93/08184 Peter Williams]

Caphouse Colliery New Road, Sitlington, West Yorkshire. SE 1648 2534
The steam winding engine was built by Davy Bros., Park Iron Works, Sheffield, in c1876 and installed new. It is a double cylinder horizontal slide valve engine with cylinder dimension of 16ins x 3 feet. The shaft is 150 yards deep and the rope drum 9 ft diameter.
[BB93/08183 Peter Williams]

Caphouse Colliery, New Road, Sitlington, West Yorkshire. SE 1648 2534
The steam winding engine.
[BB93/08179 Peter Williams]

Caphouse Colliery, New Road, Sitlington, West Yorkshire.
SE 1648 2534
The steam winding engine.
[BB93/08178 Peter Williams]

Caphouse Colliery, New Road, Sitlington, West Yorkshire. SE 1648 2534
The steam winding engine.
[BB93/08180 Peter Williams]

Caphouse Colliery, New Road, Sitlington, West Yorkshire. SE 1648 2534
The Boiler Yard with the two Lancashire boilers. [BB93/08156 Peter Williams]

Caphouse Colliery, New Road, Sitlington, West Yorkshire. SE 1648 2534
Green Lane Shaft timber headframe. [BB93/08155 Peter Williams]

Caphouse Colliery, New Road, Sitlington, West Yorkshire. SE 1648 2534
The Hope Pit Winding Engine House, Heapstead and Headgear with the Electricity Substation on the left.
[BB93/08164 Peter Williams]

Caphouse Colliery, New Road, Sitlington, West Yorkshire. SE 1648 2534
The interior of the Hope Pit Fan House. [BB93/08176 Peter Williams]

Caphouse Colliery, New Road, Sitlington, West Yorkshire. SE 1648 2534
The Hope Pit Electricity Substation. [BB93/08166 Peter Williams]

Caphouse Colliery, New Road, Sitlington, West Yorkshire. SE 1648 2534
The Hope Pit winding engine. The winder driver had acquired a fine old wooden captain's chair.
[BB93/08177 Peter Williams]

Caphouse Colliery, New Road, Sitlington, West Yorkshire. SE 1648 2534
The Hope Pit shaft head entrance. [BB93/08175 Peter Williams]

Caphouse Colliery, New Road, Sitlington, West Yorkshire. SE 1648 2534
An old tally counter, or pit check, near the staff entrance. [BB93/08154 Peter Williams]

Caphouse Colliery, New Road, Sitlington, West Yorkshire. SE 1648 2534
The conveyor from drift to screens seen through an open window.
Part of Bob Skingle's survey of 10th June 1997.
[AA97/05029 Bob Skingle]

CEAG Ltd, Pontefract Road, Barnsley, South Yorkshire.
Founded in 1906 in Cologne, CEAG is best known for its electric safety lamps. CEAG stands for Concordia Elektrizitats Aktiengesellschaft. [BB016224]

Cortonwood Colliery, Wombwell, Barnsley, South Yorkshire. SE 408 014
Although sunk in 1873, Cortonwood was but little heard of until 1984 when the NCB announced its closure together with cutbacks of 20,000 miners throughout the industry. Five months later the 1984 miners strike began. This vertical aerial photograph was taken 21st April 1953. [1437 RAF 1094 English Heritage (NMR) RAF Photography]

Front elevation
AA80/2524

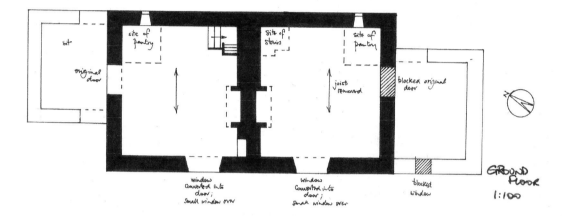

Danby Coal Mines, Clither Beck, Danby Low Moor, North Yorkshire. NZ 715 100
Centred on the farmhouse at Doubting Castle, the 'Castleton coals' are documented from the mid-18th century, being used to fire the Loftus alum pans. Seen here is a photograph and plan of Clitherbeck Cottages, thought to have been built in the late-18th century for two miner's families. Photographed 3rd August 1983. [106/56053 Ian Goodall, AA80/02524 Terry Buchanan]

Darfield Main Colliery, Darfield, Barnsley, South Yorkshire. SE 0400 4001
The colliery was sunk in 1861 and closed in 1989. This photograph was taken 26th September 1956 during surface reconstruction work. Looking west towards No.1 Shaft. [BB95/09567]

Darfield Main, Colliery, Darfield, Barnsley, South Yorkshire. SE 0400 4001
A photograph dated 30th September 1953 showing the disused winding engine. [BB95/ 09536]

Darfield Main, Colliery, Darfield, Barnsley, South Yorkshire. SE 0400 4001
Another view of the engine. Photographed 30th September 1953. [BB95/09537]

Darfield Main, Colliery, Darfield, Barnsley, South Yorkshire. SE 0400 4001
A view from the dirt stack towards the headgear. There are two sheave wheels on the headframe and from one can be seen a rope leading to the winding engine house. Further to the right can be seen the new winding engine house. Photographed 7th June 1950. [BB95/09557]

Darfield Main, Colliery, Darfield, Barnsley, South Yorkshire. SE 0400 4001
Darfield Main during surface reconstruction. The old winding engine house has been demolished and much new building has taken place. Photographed 26th September 1956. [BB95/09566]

Darfield Main, Colliery, Darfield, Barnsley, South Yorkshire. SE 0400 4001
Another view from the dirt stack. Photographed 7th June 1950. [BB95/09556]

Darfield Main, Colliery, Darfield, Barnsley, South Yorkshire. SE 0400 4001
A view of the new tipping site. Photographed 26th September 1956. [BB95/09568]

Darley Main Colliery, Worsbrough Dale, Barnsley, South Yorkshire.
Scene at the mouth of the pit after the explosion, January 1849, when 75 men and boys were killed by an explosion of 'inflammable air'. There were only 24 safety lamps available per 100 miners and on the morning of the explosion naked candles were in use. *The Illustrated London News* 3rd February 1849 page 80. [BB016201]

Worsbrough Dale, Barnsley, South Yorkshire.
The funeral of the pitmen in Worsbrough churchyard after the explosion at Darley Main Colliery in 1849. *The Illustrated London News* 3rd February 1849 page 80. [BBBB016202]

Darton Main Colliery, Darton, Barnsley, South Yorkshire. SE 310 101
The former Winding Engine House with workshops beyond. The colliery was sunk in 1914 and closed in August 1948. Photographed 27th February 1988. [61440 Anonymous donation]

Denaby Main Colliery, Denaby Main, South Yorkshire. SE 49 99
Sunk in 1863 by Denaby and Cadeby Main Collieries Ltd and closed in 1968. All that is left is the ubiquitous pit wheel set in concrete. Photographed 10th November 1993. [AA94/00347 Bob Skingle]

St Alban's Church, Denaby, Doncaster, South Yorkshire. SK 502 994
The Miners' Memorial Chapel, built in 1987 from salvaged materials. Bricks came from various pits in the area and from Mexborough Power Station. The Cadeby Colliery sheave wheel can be seen on the right hand side. The altar case contains a one ton block of coal from Manvers Main. Photographed 19th January 1993.
[AA93/01323 Bob Skingle]

St Alban's Church, Denaby, Doncaster, South Yorkshire. SK 502 994
A view from the altar. Photographed 19th January 1993.
[AA93/01320 Bob Skingle]

Deputy Row, Outwood, Wakefield, West Yorkshire.
A terrace built for colliery foremen. The part with decorative brick lozenges has only two windows to the front and its chimneys have been extended upwards, indicating that this end was built first. Photographed 21st February 1983. [YO/00740 Peter Williams]

Deputy Row, Outwood, Wakefield, West Yorkshire.
The uphill end of the terrace has houses with three windows to the front, and despite the ugly soil stacks may be of higher status. Photographed 21st February 1983. [YO/00740 Peter Williams]

The Diamond Coal-Cutter Company, Wakefield, West Yorkshire.
An advertisement from *The Colliery Managers Pocket Book* 1918.
[BB016220]

Dinnington Main Colliery, Dinnington, South Yorkshire. SK 519 868
Sunk 1901-5, the site of the colliery had been cleared by 1994 with the exception of the colliery baths and canteen, built 1932 for 3,024 men, but modified during construction for a much reduced workforce of 1,656. Photographed 24th January 1994.
[BB94/07017 Bob Skingle]

Doncaster Mines Rescue Station, Whitworth Road, Wheatley, Doncaster, South Yorkshire. SE 582 044
The station was built in1913. Photographed here 12th May 1993. [AA94/00213 Roger Thomas]

Doncaster Mines Rescue Station, Whitworth Road, Wheatley, Doncaster, South Yorkshire. SE 582 044
The lower section of the north practice gallery. Photographed 12th May 1993.
[AA94/00209 Roger Thomas]

Doncaster Mines Rescue Station, Whitworth Road, Wheatley, Doncaster, South Yorkshire. SE 582 044
The underground roadway practice gallery, dating from the 1960s. Photographed 12th May 1993.
[AA94/00208 Roger Thomas]

Doncaster Mines Rescue Station, Whitworth Road, Wheatley, Doncaster, South Yorkshire. SE 582 044
The canary aviary. Two canaries were kept at each coal mine from 1911. In 1986 some 200 birds were made
redundant by the introduction of electronic sensors. Photographed 12th May 1993. [AA94/00215 Roger Thomas]

Edmunds Main Colliery, Barnsley, South Yorkshire.
A sketch from the bank near The Masons' Arms. Coal is being loaded onto barges on the Dearne and Dove canal.
The Illustrated London News 16th July 1859. [BB016209]

Edmunds Main Colliery, Barnsley, South Yorkshire.
An explosion on the 8th December 1862 resulted in the deaths of 59 miners. A second explosion, shown here, was described as "one of the most violent that had ever occurred in the mining districts of the North". There was no loss of life, but the pit was severely damaged. *The Illustrated London News* 27th December 1862. [BB016191]

Edmunds Main Colliery, Barnsley, South Yorkshire.
The trench cut to the Dearne and the Dove canal for the purpose of flooding the pit to extinguish the fire. *The Illustrated London News* 27th December 1862. [BB016192]

Eggborough Power Station, Low Eggborough, North Yorkshire. SE 665 270

A 2GW coal fired power station commissioned in 1969, accounting for 2.5% of the England and Wales generation market. A class 58 diesel electric train on the 'merry go round' leaving the site. Photographed 12th May 1993. [AA99/ 01504 Roger Thomas]

Eggborough Power Station, Low Eggborough, North Yorkshire. SE 665 270

Dramatic sky over the cooling towers. Photographed 12th May 1993. [AA01497 Roger Thomas]

Elsecar Colliery, Elsecar, Hoyland Nether, South Yorkshire. SE 390 002
Sunk c1910 and photographed here in 1984 during closure, the site was cleared by 1987. The upcast shaft and winder are on the right and the downcast shaft in the background. [61442 Anonymous donation]

Elsecar Colliery, Elsecar, Hoyland Nether, South Yorkshire. SE 390 002
A capstan for changing the winding ropes on the main winder, photographed 1984. [61442 Anonymous donation]

Elsecar Footrill, Wentworth Road, Elsecar, Hoyland Nether, South Yorkshire.
SK 3850 9965
A pedestrian entrance to the Footrill probably built c1795 for the Fitzwilliam estate. Seen from the west. Photographed 8th January 1993. [AA93/01057 Bob Skingle]

Elsecar Footrill, Wentworth Road, Elsecar, Hoyland Nether, South Yorkshire. SK 3850 9965
The interior. Photographed 8th January 1993. [AA93/01058 Bob Skingle]

Elsecar Miners Hostel, Fitzwilliam Street, Elsecar, Hoyland Nether, South Yorkshire. SK 390 002
Built 1853, it is seen on the 18th January 1979, before conversion in 1982 when it became 14 flats called 'Fitzwilliam Lodge'. [BB81/07224 Bob Skingle]

Elsecar National Coal Board Depot, Wath, Elsecar, Hoyland Nether, South Yorkshire.
Now the Elsecar Heritage Centre. The workshop adjoining the aisled workshop, photographed 19th October 1988. [BB93/05883 Bob Skingle]

Elsecar National Coal Board Depot, Elsecar, Hoyland Nether, South Yorkshire.
The southern workshop. Photographed 19th October 1988. [BB93/05884 Bob Skingle]

The Newcomen Engine House, Elsecar, Hoyland Nether, South Yorkshire.
Sole surviving Newcomen engine *in situ*, listed grade 1. It operated as a pumping engine from c1795-1928. The datestone above the door is thought to be a contemporary mistake. Seen here in July 1961. [Strip 38 no. 12 C.F. Stell]

The Newcomen Engine House, Elsecar, Hoyland Nether, South Yorkshire.
A view taken 17th April 2003, showing the concrete headframe in the foreground. Notice how the engine pump rod frame has been changed. [AA041980 Peter Williams]

49

The Newcomen Engine House, Elsecar, Hoyland Nether, South Yorkshire.
Interior ground floor view. Photographed 8th January 1993. [AA93/01409 Bob Skingle]

The Newcomen Engine House, Elsecar, Hoyland Nether, South Yorkshire.
Modern weights balance the beam. Photographed 8th January 1993. [AA93/01407]

The Newcomen Engine House, Elsecar, Hoyland Nether, South Yorkshire.
The third floor, showing the 'new' beam of 1801. Photographed 8th January 1993. [AA93/01417]

51

Featherstone Drift drag line, Wakefield, West Yorkshire. SE 415 213
The Miller Mining Company moveable crane. Photographed 23rd November 1992. [AA92/07081 Bob Skingle]

Frickley Colliery, South Elmsall, Pontefract, West Yorkshire.
SE 445 117
Opened in 1905, extended in 1923 to include the South Elmsall mine, demolished 1993. In 1958 *The Colliery Guardian* gives the figure of 2,267 men underground and 580 above ground. Here we see the end of shift on the 28th January 1993. [AA93/02670 James O Davies]

Frickley Colliery, South Elmsall, Pontefract, West Yorkshire.
SE 445 117
Pithead baths – showering miners, the one washing the back of the other, 28th January 1993.
[AA93/03754 James O Davies]

The Miners Arms, Aberford Road, Garforth, West Yorkshire. SE 405 335
Two miners are shown with modern coal cutting equipment on a pub sign near Micklefield Garden Village and Allerton Bywater Colliery. Photographed 11th January 1993. [AA93/01004 Bob Skingle]

Awarded Silver Medal, Mining Exhibition, Glasgow, 1885.

GILLOTT'S IMPROVED

Gillott & Copley Patent Rotary Coal-cutting Machine.

WILL CUT FROM 20 YARDS PER HOUR 3 FT. 4 IN. DEEP.

Illustration of our C class Improved Machine, to work in an 18 in. seam of coal.

These Machines have, during the last four years, been entirely re-modelled and great improvements introduced, by which means we are enabled to make the Machines to cut to the end of a face, then reverse and cut back again, without moving the Machine or removing Cutter Wheel. They will cut either up or down hill, or on a level, and are constructed wholly of Crucible Cast Steel (with the exception of the cylinders), Phosphor Bronze, and Wrought Iron, and are of the very best workmanship throughout.

THREE CLASSES OR SIZES ARE MADE.

For further particulars apply to Patentees and Sole Manufacturers,

JNO. GILLOTT & SON,
BARNSLEY, YORKSHIRE.

Gillott and Copley, Barnsley, South Yorkshire.
An advertisement from *The Mechanical Engineering of Collieries* by C M Percy 1886. [AA035787]

Glass Houghton Colliery, Castleford, North Yorkshire. SE 435 244
The colliery opened in 1869 and closed 1986. The steam winding engine of 1918 built by Walker Brothers Ltd, Wigan, seen here on the 18th September 1976. [76/18/32 George Cooper]

Goldthorpe Colliery, Goldthorpe, Doncaster, South Yorkshire. SE 469 042
Sunk in 1910, the colliery first worked by a shaft. In 1958 the drift entrance was introduced, when, incidentally, the *Colliery Guardian* lists 387 men below ground and 85 above. In 1966 Goldthorpe amalgamated with the nearby Highgate Colliery. The covered conveyors can clearly be seen, sending coal to the bunker on the right. Photographed 8th September 1992. [CCX14242/14 Cox Collection, NMR]

St John & St Mary Magdalene, Lockwood Road, Goldthorpe, Dearne, Doncaster, South Yorkshire. SE 464 046
Lord Halifax commissioned the architect Alfred Nutt to design this remarkable ferro-concrete church and vicarage in 1916, to serve the Hickleton Main Colliery community. Photographed 10th February 2004.
[AA046211 Peter Williams]

No.3 Compartment Boat Hoist, Goole Docks, Aire Street, Goole, Humberside. SE 7463 2329
The No 3 Hoist was built 1889 by the Aire and Calder Navigation Company. One of five similar hoists, the earliest of which was built 1862, only No 5 now remains complete. The hoists were used to transfer coal from the Tom Pudding barges into sea-going vessels. Photographed as part of an extensive survey of the docks, 9th November 1993. [AA93/04761 Roger Thomas]

Grimethorpe Colliery, Brierley, South Yorkshire. SE 410 085
The first sods were turned on Monday 8th October 1894 by J H Turner, general manager of the Midland Railway Company and Joseph Mitchell JP, senior partner in the Mitchell Main Colliery Company. Grimethorpe is best known for its Brass Band and also as the location of 'Grimley' in the film *Brassed Off*. The view shown here is titled 'new roadway' and is dated 30th July 1959. [BB95/09507]

Grimethorpe Colliery, Brierley, South Yorkshire. SE 410 085
A view taken 21st March 1961 during post-nationalisation reconstruction, showing the demolition of old screens. [BB95/09525]

Grimethorpe Colliery, Brierley, South Yorkshire. SE 410 085
An oblique aerial view of the extensive industrial landscape of the Grimethorpe site. Taken 18th January 1993, this view from the south shows the colliery to the southeast of the twin chimneys of the power station. To the south of the colliery is the site of Carlton Main Brickworks and Pulverite Works. To the southwest of the cooling tower is the vast smokeless fuel and chemical works. [NMR 12351/30]

Grimethorpe Colliery, Brierley, South Yorkshire. SE 410 085
Another view,18th January 1993, this time from the north. The 'underground landscape' at Grimethorpe is, presumably, every bit as complex as that seen from the air. To the left of the cooling tower is the site of the former Ferrymoor Colliery. In 1963 Grimethorpe amalgamated with Houghton Main and the output of both mines was raised at Grimethorpe. Sixteen seams were exploited using three shafts, which were infilled and capped in 1994. [NMR 12351/37]

Grimethorpe Colliery, Brierley, South Yorkshire. SE 410 085
An undated photograph showing surface reconstruction – unloading a fan rotor. [BB95/09504]

Grimethorpe Colliery, Brierley, South Yorkshire. SE 410 085
The Koepe tower with garden. Photographed 23 June 1961. [BB95/09531]

A Halifax Coal Pit.
An illustration of a female hurrier in a Halifax Coal Pit, from *Tomlinsons Cyclopaedia of Useful Arts*, 1854. Tomlinson describes the methods of working in coal mines before the *Coal Mines Act* of March 1843 made it illegal to employ females or boys under the age of ten below ground:

> "The corves drawn by the hurriers weigh from 2 to 5 cwt: they are mounted on four cast-iron wheels, 5 inches in diameter, but not moving on rails. The corves are dragged by children through passages in some cases not more than from 16 to 20 inches in height: they buckle round their naked persons a broad leather strap, which is attached in front to a ring and about 4 feet of chain, terminating in a hook." [AA035530]

Opposite page: Hadfield's Steel Foundry Company, Attercliffe, Sheffield, South Yorkshire.
An advertisement from *The Mechanical Engineering of Collieries* by C M Percy 1886. Sir Robert Abbott Hadfield developed manganese steel c1882-8. By 1919 Hadfield's was Sheffield's biggest employer. [BB016206]

Harrison and Camm Ltd, Rotherham, South Yorkshire.
An advertisement from *The Colliery Managers Pocket Book* 1918. [BB016215]

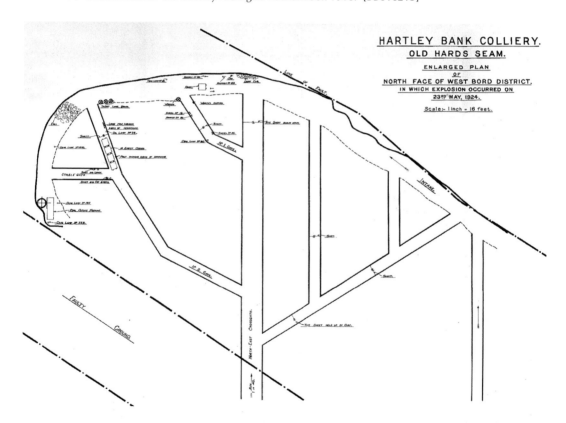

Hartley Bank Colliery, Horbury, Netherton, Sitlington, West Yorkshire. SE 286 173
On the 23rd May 1924 an explosion occurred in the Old Hards Seam. Four people lost their lives and two others were injured. The cause of the explosion was thought to be a sparking commutator on the coal cutting machine igniting concentrated firedamp. The underground plan shown is taken from the official *Report on the Explosion of 1924* by Henry Walker. Hartley Bank is perhaps best known for the bravery of James Gillan who was awarded the George Medal 31st October 1959. [BB016213]

Hatfield Colliery, Stainforth, South Yorkshire. SE 653 112
Two shafts were sunk between 1911 and 1921 by the Hatfield Main Colliery Company Limited. Difficulty was encountered in sinking due to sand overlying waterlogged sandstone. Piling was used to get through the sand and the Francois cementation process used in the sandstone. In 1986 the colliery was merged with Thorne Colliery via an underground link. NCB closure came in December 1993. The Hatfield Coal Company took over but went into receivership in 2001, when Coal Power took over. This view shows the winding engine houses and powerhouse from the southwest. Photographed 4th May 1993. [AA94/00374 Keith Buck]

Hatfield Colliery, Stainforth, South Yorkshire. SE 653 112
The latticework headgear to No.1 shaft in the foreground was built by Naylor Bros of Golbourne, Lancashire. The No.2 shaft headgear beyond was a ferro-concrete design by the Trussed Concrete Steel Company Limited. Photographed 4th May 1993. [AA94/00373 Keith Buck]

Hatfield Colliery. Stainforth, South Yorkshire. SE 653 112
The pithead baths, built 1934 by the Miners' Welfare Fund. Photographed 4th May 1993. [AA94/00351 Keith Buck]

Hatfield Colliery, Stainforth, South Yorkshire. SE 653 112
The fan house and No.2 heapstead. Photographed 4th May 1993. [AA94/00371 Keith Buck]

HATHORN DAVEY & CO.,
SUN FOUNDRY,
LEEDS.

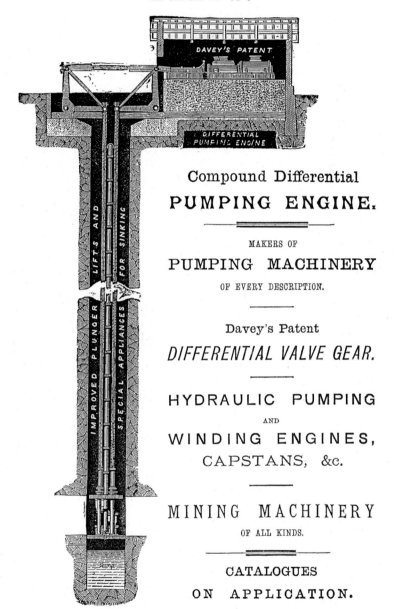

Compound Differential
PUMPING ENGINE.

MAKERS OF
PUMPING MACHINERY
OF EVERY DESCRIPTION.

Davey's Patent
DIFFERENTIAL VALVE GEAR.

HYDRAULIC PUMPING
AND
WINDING ENGINES,
CAPSTANS, &c.

MINING MACHINERY
OF ALL KINDS.

CATALOGUES
ON APPLICATION.

Hathorn Davey & Company, Sun Foundry, Leeds, West Yorkshire.
An advertisement from *The Mechanical Engineering of Collieries* by C M Percy 1886. The Sun Foundry dates from 1846 and until 1872 the proprietors were Carrett Marshall and Company. Hathorn then took over, Henry Davey joining in 1874. The firm concentrated on Davey's non-rotative pumping engines. Subsequently it became a subsidiary of Sulzers. [908499 3.10.5]

Hay Royd Colliery, Sitlington, West Yorkshire. SE 2868 1572
A general view of the drift mine established 1908 and operated by the Flack family as a licensed pit. Photographed 26th January 1993. [AA93/02684 James O Davies]

Hay Royd Colliery, Sitlington, West Yorkshire. SE 2868 1572
At pit bottom. Photographed 26th January 1993. [AA93/02689 James O Davies]

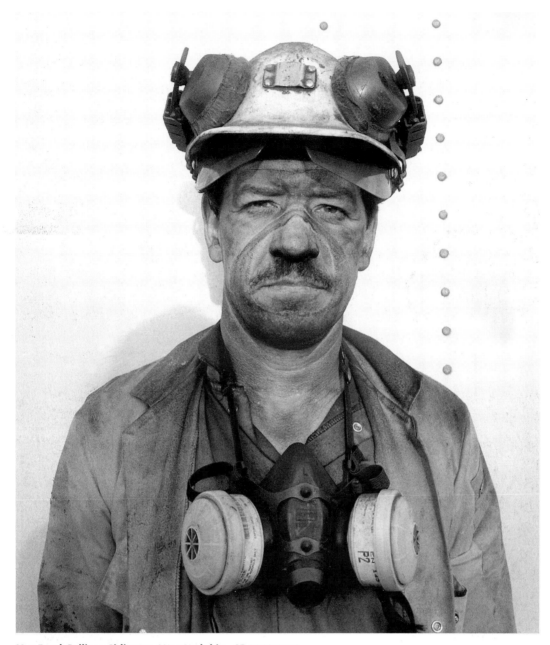

Hay Royd Colliery, Sitlington, West Yorkshire. SE 2868 1572
At end of shift. Photographed 26th January 1993. [AA93/02688 James O Davies]

Hay Royd Colliery, Sitlington, West Yorkshire. SE 2868 1572
Barry Sharpe at end of shift. Photographed 26th January 1993. [AA93/02687 James O Davies]

Hemingfield Colliery, Elsecar, Hoyland Nether, South Yorkshire. SE 392 010
Part of the Fitzwilliam Estate, the colliery was sunk in 1842 and closed in 1920, although it continued to be used for drainage. As late as 1988, when these photographs were taken, the buildings were still in remarkable condition. [61441 Anonymous donation.]

Hemingfield Colliery, Elsecar, Hoyland Nether, South Yorkshire. SE 392 010
A stubby concrete headframe on the right, a two storey winding house in the centre and a three storey sandstone house on the left. Photographed in 1988. [61441 Anonymous donation.]

Hickleton Main Colliery, Thurnscoe, Dearne, Barnsley, South Yorkshire. SE 465 053
Sunk 1892-3, merged with Goldthorpe Colliery in 1986, closed 1988. Here we see the pit wheel memorial erected in 1993. Photographed 10th November 1993. [AA94/00342 Bob Skingle]

Hickleton Main Colliery, Thurnscoe, Dearne, Barnsley, South Yorkshire. SE 465 053
A view from the southwest. Photographed 11th May 1993. [AA94/00308 Keith Buck]

Hickleton Main Colliery, Thurnscoe, Dearne, Barnsley, South Yorkshire. SE 465 053
The No.3 Shaft dating to c1921, a latticework steel structure later encased in ferro-concrete. Photographed 11th May 1993. [AA94/00313 Keith Buck]

Hickleton Main Colliery, Thurnscoe, Dearne, Barnsley, South Yorkshire. SE 465 053
The drift entrance. Photographed 11th May 1993. [AA94/00311 Keith Buck]

Hickleton Main Colliery, Thurnscoe, Dearne, Barnsley, South Yorkshire. SE 465 053
The portal of the Shafton drift. Photographed 11th May 1993. [AA94/00312 Keith Buck]

Hickleton Main Colliery, Thurnscoe, Dearne, Barnsley, South Yorkshire. SE 465 053
The winding engine house, No.3 Shaft. Built by the Hickleton Main Colliery Company c1921. Photographed 11th May 1993. [AA94/00317 Keith Buck]

Hickleton Main Colliery, Thurnscoe, Dearne, Barnsley, South Yorkshire. SE 465 053
The steam winding engine, manufactured by Markham and Co Ltd, Chesterfield in 1921. Photographed 11th May 1993. [AA94/00303 Keith Buck]

Hickleton Main Colliery, Thurnscoe, Dearne, Barnsley, South Yorkshire. SE 465 053
The controls of the steam winding engine. Photographed 11th May 1993. [AA94/00310 Keith Buck]

Hickleton Main Colliery, Thurnscoe, Dearne, Barnsley, South Yorkshire. SE 465 053
The winding engine house steam wincher. The chains hang down from the travelling crane built by Middleton Brothers of Pudsey. Photographed 11th May 1993. [AA94/00309 Keith Buck]

Hickleton Main Colliery, Thurnscoe, Dearne, Barnsley, South Yorkshire. SE 465 053
The interior of the control cabin, in the Shafton drift winder-house. Photographed 11th May 1993.
[AA94/00302 Keith Buck]

Hollin Busk Colliery and Fireclay Mine, Hollin Busk Lane, Stocksbridge, South Yorkshire. SK 276 973
A view looking north towards Stocksbridge. Interesting rusty ironwork lies around the site which is not far from The Miners Arms public house. Photographed 10th February 2004.
[AA046209 Peter Williams]

Houghton Main Colliery, Little Houghton, South Yorkshire. SE 420 062

Sinking began c1870. Figures for 1957 give 1,542 underground workers and 387 above ground. The colliery closed in the winter of 1992-93 with the loss of 440 jobs. Shown here is a copy of an undated old photograph. The rocky area on the lower right hand side is where the pithead baths were to be built in 1931. Also absent from the centre of the photograph is the No.3 shaft, built between 1924 and 1933. *A Colliery Guardian* plan of the site, 6th January 1933, shows the building to the lower left to be the power house and beyond it, the No.2 battery of Lancashire boilers. In the centre is the loco shed with the No.1 battery of Lancashire boilers beyond. No.1 shaft is to the right and No.2 to the left. The wagons appear to be RCH design c1900. Six lads look up at the photographer. [AA93/03437]

Houghton Main Colliery, Little Houghton, South Yorkshire. SE 420 062
A photograph dated 1958 showing the pithead area, with No.1 Shaft to left. [AA93/ 03442]

Houghton Main Colliery, Little Houghton, South Yorkshire. SE 420 062
Another photograph dated 1958 showing No.3 Shaft winder house and headgear. [AA93/03459]

Houghton Main Colliery, Little Houghton, South Yorkshire. SE 420 062
The headgear of No.1 Shaft from the southwest. Photographed in 1958. [AA93/03441]

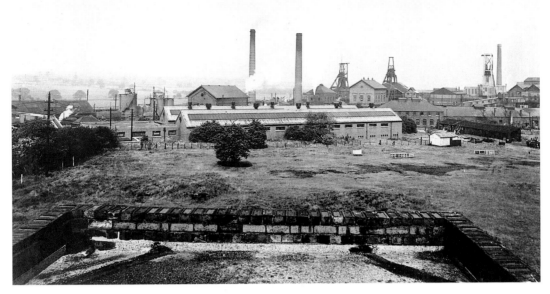

Houghton Main Colliery, Little Houghton, South Yorkshire. SE 420 062
A photograph dated 1950s from the southeast. [AA93/03438]

Houghton Main Colliery, Little Houghton, South Yorkshire. SE 420 062
The pit site from the southeast. Photographed in 1985. [AA93/03440]

Houghton Main Colliery, Little Houghton, South Yorkshire. SE 420 062
A photograph dated 1954, showing the No.1 Shaft steam winder from the
south. Built by Davy Bros. Park Ironworks, Sheffield. [AA93/03460]

Houghton Main Colliery, Little Houghton, South Yorkshire. SE 420 062
The No.1 electric replacement winder built by Robey and Co.Ltd., Lincoln [No. MO 53659]. Photographed 6th
May 1993. [AA93/03085 Keith Buck]

Houghton Main Colliery, Little Houghton, South Yorkshire. SE 420 062
No.1 headgear and the winding house seen from the south. Photographed 6th May 1993. [AA93/03069 Keith Buck]

Houghton Main Colliery, Little Houghton, South Yorkshire. SE 420 062
No.3 headgear and heapstead seen from the west. Photographed 6th May 1993. [AA93/03051 Keith Buck]

Houghton Main Colliery, Little Houghton, South Yorkshire. SE 420 062
The disused fan house, No.3 Shaft, seen from the north. Photographed 6th May 1993. [AA93/03049 Keith Buck]

Houghton Main Colliery, Little Houghton, South Yorkshire. SE 420 062
The lamp cabin dating from 1900-20, subsequently used as a lecture room, gas testing room and a fire station. The walkway was introduced c1940-50 to improve circulation of miners through the checking room at shift change. Photographed 6th May 1993. [AA93/03077 Keith Buck]

Houghton Main Colliery, Little Houghton, South Yorkshire. SE 420 062
The pithead baths were opened on the 24th January 1931 by Emmanuel Shinwell MP, Secretary for Mines, supported by General Sir J F Laycock and T W Illsley J P Built by the Miners Welfare Fund at a cost of £25,000. The baths had 2,016 of each locker type and 90 shower cubicles. Detailed instructions were provided for each miner on the wet locker/dry locker system:

"Causes of clothes not drying:
1. Vest hung up inside shirt, therefore only shirt is dried.
2. Clothes flung on bottom of locker. Therefore heat cannot rise and only the garment at bottom is dried.
3. Ventilation not properly regulated by attendants."

Further suggestions were made concerning the use of sandals in the baths. "Wooden sandals could be made by the men without any difficulty, all that is necessary being two pieces of wood, shaped roughly to the sole of the foot and a piece of webbing or strap nailed across the top, under which the front part of the foot is passed."
A Suggestion Box was to be provided: "The management will be glad to receive sensible suggestions, but only if they are signed." The photograph, 6th May 1993, shows a view of the exterior of the pithead baths and the Medical Centre which was added in the 1950s. [AA93/03071 Keith Buck]

Houghton Main Colliery, Little Houghton, South Yorkshire. SE 420 062
The pithead baths shower room. Photographed 6th May 1993. [AA93/03054 Keith Buck]

Houghton Main Colliery, Little Houghton, South Yorkshire. SE 420 062
Pihead baths dirty locker room. Photographed 6th May 1993. [AA 93/03082 Keith Buck]

Houghton Main Colliery, Little Houghton, South Yorkshire. SE 420 062
The No.5 boot room. Photographed 6th May 1993. [AA95/01974 Keith Buck]

Houghton Main Colliery, Little Houghton, South Yorkshire.
SE 420 062
A photograph dated 1961 showing the No.2 Shaft Koepe tower under construction, with the older headgear still in place beneath it.
[AA93/03455]

Houghton Main Colliery, Little Houghton, South Yorkshire.
SE 420 062
The Koepe winder tower to No.2 Shaft. The winding engine was built by David Brown, with an 850hp D.C. electric motor by Metropolitan-Vickers. Photographed 6th May 1993. [AA93/03079 Keith Buck]

HUDSWELL, CLARKE & CO. LD.,
Railway Foundry, LEEDS.

Tel. Address : "LOCO, LEEDS."

Tel. No. 3540.

LOCOMOTIVE
TANK ENGINES
OF ALL SIZES AND ANY GAUGE OF RAILWAY.

Of greatly improved construction for Main or Branch Railways, Contractors, Ironworks, Collieries.

Sole Makers of "Rodgers'" Pulleys (Reg.). **Wrought Iron throughout, Rim, Arms and Boss.**

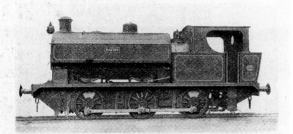
Hudswell Clarke and Company Limited, Railway Foundry, Leeds, West Yorkshire.
An advertisement from *The Colliery Managers Pocket Book* 1918. The Company built locomotives from 1861 on the site of the works of E B Wilson. It traded 1870-80 as Hudswell Clarke and Rodgers. The last engine was built 30th October 1967. [BB016219]

The Hunslet Engine Company, Leeds, West Yorkshire.
An advertisement from *The Colliery Managers Pocket Book* 1918. Founded 1860 as a general engineering company, Hunslet began production of steam locomotives c1864. The flameproof diesel locomotives were produced from 1925. The last steam locomotive was built in 1961. The company took over Manning Wardle in 1927, Kerr Stuart & Co in 1930, Avonside Engine Co in 1934 and Andrew Barclay in 1972. It also absorbed Kitson & Co and Hudswell Clarke. [BB016216]

Husker Pit Disaster Memorial, All Saints Church, High Street, Silkstone, South Yorkshire. SE 29 06
Twenty six boys and girls were killed at Husker pit, Moorend Lane, Knabbs Wood, Silkstone Common on the 4th of July 1838 when a thunderstorm flooded the day hole. The tragic events at this pit led to the setting up of the Children's Employment Commission of 1842 and the subsequent prohibition of the employment of women and girls in mines. Photographed 23rd November 1992. [AA92/07082 Bob Skingle]

Therefore be ye also ready.
Matthew XXIV Chap. 44 Verse

The mortal remains of the Females are deposited in the Graves at the feet of the Males as undernamed,
1st Grave begining at the South end,
Catharine Garnett Aged 11 Years.
Hannah Webster Aged 13 Years.
Elizabeth Carr Aged 13 Years.
Ann Moss Aged 9 Years.
2nd Grave,
Elizabeth Hollings Aged 15 Years.
Ellen Parker Aged 15 Years.
Hannah Taylor Aged 17 Years.
3rd Grave,
Mary Sellors Aged 10 Years.
Elizabeth Clarkson Aged 11 Years,
She lies at the feet of her Brother James Clarkson.
Sarah Newton Aged 8 Years.
Sarah Jukes Aged 10 Years.

Husker Pit Disaster Memorial. All Saints Church, High Street, Silkstone, South Yorkshire. SE 29 06
A detail of the side of the Memorial with the names of the girls killed. Photographed 23rd November 1992.
[AA93/01061 Bob Skingle]

Kellingley Colliery, Beal, Selby, North Yorkshire. SE 528 238
Known locally as 'The big K', the colliery was constructed from new in 1958. Shown here is the Union Banner, photographed at the Durham Miners' Gala, 13th July 2002. [AA035602 Peter Williams]

Kellingley Colliery, Beal, Selby, North Yorkshire. SE 528 238
A view of the washing and preparation plant from the south. Photographed 19th November 1992.
[AA92/07110 Bob Skingle]

Kellingley Colliery, Beal, Selby, North Yorkshire. SE 528 238
A view from east southeast with a class 56 train in the foreground. Photographed 24th January 1993.
[AA93/01440 Bob Skingle]

Kiveton Park Colliery, Wales, South Yorkshire. SK 493 826
The first shaft was sunk in 1866, coal being taken by rail to Grimsby and Hull on the Great Central Railway of 1845. Amalgamation with Sherwood Colliery took place in 1928 and Kiveton Park was taken over by The United Steel Co. in 1944. Closure came in 1994. The photograph shows the site from the south, 7th May 1993.
[AA94/00224 Keith Buck]

Kiveton Park Colliery, Wales, South Yorkshire. SK 493 826
The Power House dates from 1915. Colliery buildings seen from the south. Photographed 7th May 1993.
[AA94/00221 Keith Buck]

Kiveton Park Colliery, Wales, South Yorkshire. SK 493 826
The Colliery Offices were built between 1872 and 1875 and are listed grade II. On the north side is a Memorial to the 61 Kiveton men who died in the First World War. Photographed 7th May 1993.
[AA94/00238 Keith Buck]

Kiveton Park Colliery, Wales, South Yorkshire. SK 493 826
The pithead baths, canteen and medical centre were built by the Miners' Welfare Fund in 1936-38, designed by the architect W.A.Woodland in modernist style and are listed grade II. Photographed 7th May 1993. [AA94/00237 Keith Buck]

Kiveton Park Colliery, Wales, South Yorkshire. SK 493 826
The headgear to No.1 Shaft. Photographed 7th May 1993. The headgear was erected in 1964.
[AA94/00226 Keith Buck]

Kiveton Park Colliery, Wales, South Yorkshire. SK 493 826
The heapstead to No.1 Shaft, showing the north entrance to the shaft portal surviving from the original sinking.
Photographed 7th May 1993. [AA94/00228 Keith Buck]

Kiveton Park Colliery, Wales, South Yorkshire. SK 493 826
The former narrow guage locomotive shed, subsequently used as a union office and rescue centre. A bird looks
forlornly out of the ramshackle aviary on the right. Photographed 7th May 1993. [AA94/00240 Keith Buck]

Kiveton Park Colliery, Wales, South Yorkshire. SK 493 826
The No.2 Shaft heapstead and headgear date from the mid-1930s and were built of ferro-concrete. In front can be seen the fanhouse dating from 1964. Photographed 7th May 1993. [AA94/00222 Keith Buck]

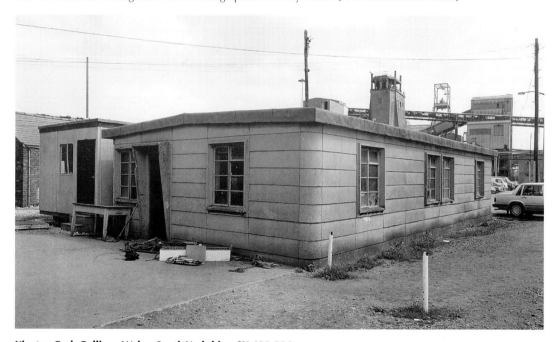

Kiveton Park Colliery, Wales, South Yorkshire. SK 493 826
The prefabricated concrete workshop and stores were originally erected as the colliery record office. Photographed 7th May 1993. [AA94/00229 Keith Buck]

Ledston Luck Colliery, Barnsdale Road, Ledston, nr Kippax, North Yorkshire. SE 431 307
A general view, 12th December 1987. [86549 Anonymous donation]

Ledston Luck Colliery, Barnsdale Road, Ledston, nr Kippax, North Yorkshire. SE 431 307
A general view, 12th December 1987. [86549 Anonymous donation]

Ledston Luck Colliery, Barnsdale Road, Ledston, nr Kippax, North Yorkshire. SE 431 307
The steel framed headgear. Photographed 12th December 1987. [86549 Anonymous donation]

Ledston Luck Colliery, Barnsdale Road, Ledston, nr Kippax, North Yorkshire. SE 431 307
The concrete constructed winding gear on the west side. Photographed 8th August 1988.
[BB91/21095 Bob Skingle]

Ledston Luck Colliery, Barnsdale Road, Ledston, nr Kippax, North Yorkshire. SE 431 307
The west winding house and winding gear with the garden wall and gate, listed grade II. Photographed 8th August 1988. [BB91/21091 Bob Skingle]

Ledston Luck Colliery, Barnsdale Road, Ledston, nr Kippax, North Yorkshire. SE 431 307
The west winding room. Photographed 8th August 1988. [BB91/21088 Bob Skingle]

Ledston Luck Colliery, Barnsdale Road, Ledston, nr Kippax, North Yorkshire.
SE 431 307
The east winding room. Photographed 8th August 1988. [BB91/21083 Bob Skingle]

Ledston Luck Colliery, Barnsdale Road, Ledston, nr Kippax, North Yorkshire.
SE 431 307
The east electric winding engine in 1988. Ledston was one of the first Yorkshire collieries to install electric winders. [BB91/21080 Bob Skingle]

Lindley Pit, Huddersfield, West Yorkshire. SE 11 18
An illustration showing Susan Pitchforth, aged 11, a hurrier at Messrs. Waterhouse in 1841. (from *The Playbook of Metals* by John Henry Pepper 8th Ed 1885 – the original version being illustration number 10 in the CEC report). Evidence for the Children's Employment Commission was taken at this pit by Samuel S Scriven on the 7th May 1841.

Susan Pitchforth
"I have been working in this pit for two years. I have been at Sunday School at Elland but never went to a day school and can read only in my A B C. I come to work at eight or before but I set off from home at seven. I live about a mile and a half from the pit. I walk a mile and a half to work and a mile and a half from my work both in winter and summer. I get porridge for breakfast before I come and bring my dinner with me, a muffin. When I have done about 12 loads. I eat it while at work. I run 24 corves a day. I can't come up till I have done them all. If I want to relieve myself I go to any part of the pit. Sometimes the boys see when they go by. My father slaps me sometimes upon the head or upon the back, so as to make me cry. I had rather set cards or anything else than work in the pit. I have one sister going of 14 and she works with me in the pit. I am a thruster. I never wore a belt. I got this cut upon my nose in the pit by falling on the shale. My feet are not very sound from having trod upon the coals and stones. They have been crushed. When I go home I get some tea and am very tired. There is plenty of blackdamp in the pit and on Monday the men could not get in from the hurriers leaving a trap door open."

Samuel S Scriven
"A very ignorant child. She stood shivering before me from cold. The rag that hung about her waist was once called a shift which is as black as the coal she thrusts and saturated with water, the drippings of the roof and shaft. During my examination of her, the banksman whom I left in the pit came to the public house and wanted to take her away because as he expressed himself it was not decent that she should be [her person] exposed to us. Oh, no! it was criminal above ground and like the two or three other colliers in the cabin, he became evidently mortified that these deeds of darkness should be brought to light." [AA035761]

Lofthouse Colliery Memorial, Wrenthorpe, Rothwell, West Yorkshire. SE 303 223

The memorial to seven men who drowned on the 21st March 1973 when a coal cutter broke into old workings at Lofthouse Colliery South 9B face and water flooded in. The newly elected Area Compensation Agent, Arthur Scargill, established the liability of the Coal Board, in failing to take heed of records kept by the Institute of Geological Sciences, Leeds. The subsequent emergence of a more militant Yorkshire Union contributed to the 1974 strike and the defeat of Edward Heath's Conservative government. Photographed 23rd November 1992. [AA92/07077 Bob Skingle]

Lofthouse Colliery Memorial, Wrenthorpe, Rothwell, West Yorkshire. SE 303 223

The Wrenthorpe area, known for its pottery industry and later for colliery rope and twine manufacture, was surrounded by old workings. Amongst the many long closed mines were Smithson's Colliery, The Stanley Victoria Colliery and Wrenthorpe Colliery. Lofthouse closed in 1981. Detail of the base of the memorial. Photographed 23rd November 1992. [AA92/07079 Bob Skingle]

Long Row, New Sharlston, West Yorkshire. SE 383 204
Twenty nine through cottages and twenty six back to backs (No.s 30-43) were built by the New Sharlston Colliery Company between 1865 and 1870. The involvement of the Crossley family from West Hill Park led to the local provision of a chapel, school, penny bank, reading room and co-operative store. A view from the southeast. Photographed 21st February 1983. [YO 742 Peter Williams]

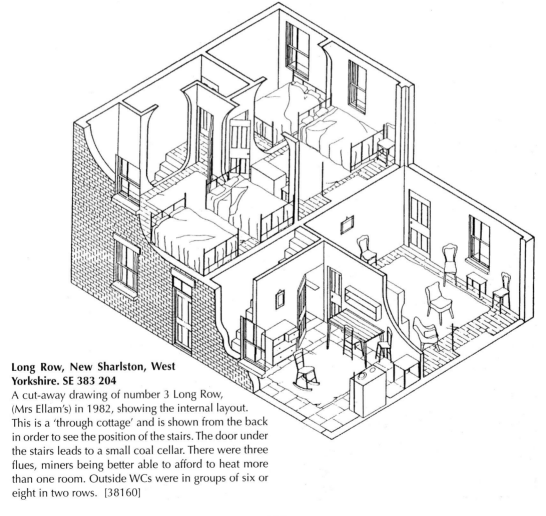

Long Row, New Sharlston, West Yorkshire. SE 383 204
A cut-away drawing of number 3 Long Row, (Mrs Ellam's) in 1982, showing the internal layout. This is a 'through cottage' and is shown from the back in order to see the position of the stairs. The door under the stairs leads to a small coal cellar. There were three flues, miners being better able to afford to heat more than one room. Outside WCs were in groups of six or eight in two rows. [38160]

Lundhill Colliery, Wombwell, Nr. Barnsley, South Yorkshire.
Shortly after mid-day on the 19th February 1857 one hundred and eighty nine men and boys lost their lives after
an explosion at Taylor and Co.'s Lundhill Colliery. *The Illustrated London News* 7th March 1857. [BB016189]

Lundhill Colliery, Wombwell, Nr. Barnsley, South Yorkshire.
The mouth of the downcast shaft after it had been blocked to close off the air to the fire below. The iron basket , or corve, in which the miners made their descent is seen at the top. Feeding in from the left is the steam pipe used in an inadequate attempt to extinguish the fire, whilst in the foreground is the brick tank lined with charcoal preparatory to making carbonic acid gas, for the same purpose. Water from a neighbouring stream was subsequently fed into the mine. *The Illustrated London News* 7th March 1857. [BB016190]

Lundhill Colliery, Wombwell, Nr Barnsley, South Yorkshire.
The scene of the explosion. *The Illustrated London News* correspondent:

"Every train to-day has brought a large number of "excursionists" who by their conduct seemed bound to a fair or country fête rather than visitors to the scene of a frightful calamity. Each road leading to the pit was covered with throngs of people, dotting the highway for miles in every direction; and the immediate neighbourhood of the works could only be compared to Greenwich-hill on a summer Sunday. At two o'clock there were from 10,000 to 15,000 persons on the spot; and few indeed were those who appeared to think they were standing immediately over the bodies of nearly 200 human beings, hurried without a moments notice into eternity. In the dense crowd before them the loud laugh and jest were heard incessantly. It is true there was little to indicate what had taken place beyond a heap of rubbish and boards a few feet high over the cupola shaft, from which a white smoke was issuing in small quantity; but the larger part of the crowd were neighbouring pitmen, pitmen's wives and children; and it is difficult to understand the callousness of their conduct, contrasted with that of a few grouped round an individual who was "improving the occasion" their voices raised occasionally in hymns which swelled and murmured over the confused Babel with an effect that may be imagined, but not described. There was only one spot which spoke of death – the interior of the building over the downcast shaft, black and grim with coaldust; a grey light stealing through the timbers from the roof, and lighting it mysteriously; made more sad by a few bright spots of sunbeam which danced upon the walls here and there; while a broader gleam hung upon the now useless cradle in which the unfortunate miners had made their last descent – a shovel here, a bucket there – and nought of life, but the hissing of the steam as it escaped from the pipe down which it was forced through the covering of the shaft, for the purpose of extinguishing the fire."

The Illustrated London News, 28th February 1857. [BB016188]

Lundhill Colliery Explosion Memorial, Church Street, Darfield, South Yorkshire. SE 415 043
The monument by W Oxley of Barnsley, was erected in 1857. Photographed 19th November 1992.
[AA92/07010 Bob Skingle]

Maltby Colliery, Tickhill Road, Maltby, South Yorkshire. SK 551 924
The banner of the NUM Maltby Branch, seen at the Durham Miners' Gala on the 13th July 2002. [AA035597 Peter Williams]

Maltby Colliery, Tickhill Road, Maltby, South Yorkshire. SK 551 924
Sunk 1908, the mine came into production in 1911, being developed by the Maltby Main Colliery Company, a subsidiary of the Sheepbridge Iron and Coal Company Limited. Ownership then passed to Amalgamated Denaby Collieries Limited and then to Yorkshire Amalgamated Collieries Limited. A major reworking of the site took place 1951-61 and again in 1981, for the 'Parkgate Project'. Shown here is a copy of a photograph, taken 11th August 1958, of No.1 pithead [left] and No.2 pithead [right]. [BB94/12586]

Maltby Colliery, Tickhill Road, Maltby, South Yorkshire. SK 551 924
No.1 pithead. Photographed 2nd August 1958. [BB94/12607]

Maltby Colliery, Tickhill Road, Maltby, South Yorkshire. SK 551 924
No.1 winding house. Photographed 7th July 1958. [BB94/12612]

Maltby Colliery, Tickhill Road, Maltby, South Yorkshire. SK 551 924
No.1 heapstead during demolition on 5th August 1958. [BB94/12608]

Maltby Colliery, Tickhill Road, Maltby, South Yorkshire. SK 551 924
Tubway gantry. Photographed 6th August 1958. [BB94/12593]

Maltby Colliery, Tickhill Road, Maltby, South Yorkshire. SK 551 924
No.1 pithead. Photographed 1st August 1958. [BB94/12610]

Maltby Colliery, Tickhill Road, Maltby, South Yorkshire. SK 551 924
Coal preparation area and marshalling yard. Photographed 8th August 1958. [BB94/12601]

Maltby Colliery, Tickhill Road, Maltby, South Yorkshire. SK 551 924
No.1 pithead. Photographed 7th October 1958. [BB94/12594]

Maltby Colliery, Tickhill Road, Maltby, South Yorkshire. SK 551 924
No. 1 winding engine. Photographed 29th January 1958. The original horizontal twin cylinder steam winding engine was built 1910 by Markham and Company of Chesterfield. It was replaced by a Markham AC1725 HP Electric winder in 1958. [BB94/07084]

Maltby Colliery, Tickhill Road, Maltby, South Yorkshire. SK 551 924
No.1 winding engine. Photographed 30th July 1958. [BB94/12597]

Maltby Colliery, Tickhill Road, Maltby, South Yorkshire. SK 551 924
The No.3 Koepe winder tower under construction, 9th August 1986. Some 270 feet high it is built of ferro-concrete using the continuous casting process. Four 25 ton skips are worked by two 4,000HP electric winders. The No. 3 Shaft is 3,250 feet deep to the Parkgate seam and the raising capacity amounts to 1,200 tonnes per hour. [BB94/07079]

Maltby Colliery, Tickhill Road, Maltby, South Yorkshire. SK 551 924
The No. 3 Koepe winding tower from the west. Photographed 5th May 1993. [AA94/00251 Keith Buck]

Maltby Colliery, Tickhill Road, Maltby, South Yorkshire. SK 551 924
The No. 3 Koepe winding tower electric winders. Photographed 5th May 1993. [AA94/00283 Keith Buck]

Maltby Colliery, Tickhill Road, Maltby, South Yorkshire. SK 551 924
No.1 winding engine house, heapstead and headgear. The lattice steel headgear dates from 1911. Photographed 5th May 1993. [AA94/00255 Keith Buck]

Maltby Colliery, Tickhill Road, Maltby, South Yorkshire. SK 551 924
No.1 winding engine. Photographed 5th May 1993. [AA94/00259 Keith Buck]

Maltby Colliery, Tickhill Road, Maltby, South Yorkshire. SK 551 924
The interior of the power house of 1910-11. Photographed 5th May 1993. [AA94/00257 Keith Buck]

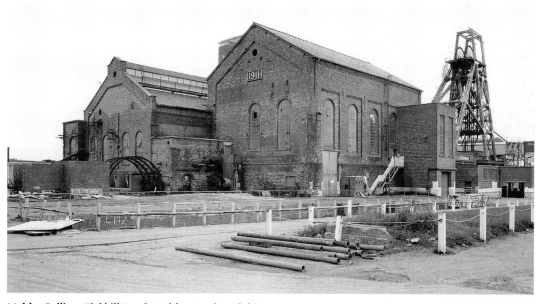

Maltby Colliery. Tickhill Road, Maltby, South Yorkshire. SK 551 924
The power house and No.1 winding engine house. Photographed 5th May 1993. [AA94/00272 Keith Buck]

Maltby Colliery, Tickhill Road, Maltby, South Yorkshire. SK 551 924
The lamp cabin from the west. Photographed 5th May 1993. [AA94/00281 Keith Buck]

Maltby Colliery. Tickhill Road, Maltby, South Yorkshire. SK 551 924
The raised walkway from the lamp cabin to the pit. Photographed 5th May 1993. [AA94/00275 Keith Buck]

Maltby Colliery, Tickhill Road, Maltby, South Yorkshire. SK 551 924
A general view from the north with the pithead baths in the centre. The baths and canteen were built 1937-38 by the Miners Welfare Fund, Architect W.A.Woodland, for a workforce of 2,496 men. Photographed 5th May 1993. [AA94/00264 Keith Buck]

Maltby Colliery, Tickhill Road, Maltby, South Yorkshire. SK 551 924
The coal bunker dates from the late 1980s and was built as part of the Parkgate Scheme. Photographed 5th May 1993. [AA94/00285 Keith Buck]

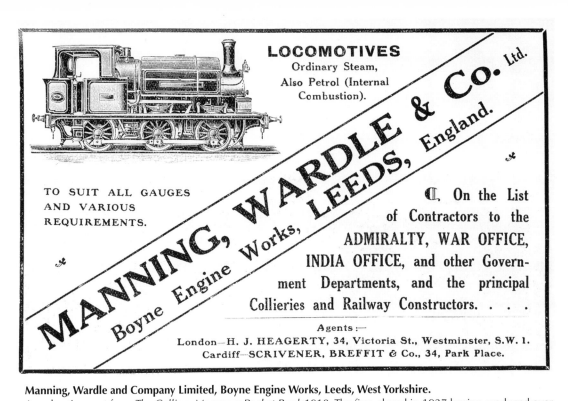

Manning, Wardle and Company Limited, Boyne Engine Works, Leeds, West Yorkshire.
An advertisement from *The Colliery Managers Pocket Book* 1918. The firm closed in 1927 having produced over 2,000 steam locomotives. [BB016218]

Manvers Main Colliery, Wath upon Dearne, South Yorkshire. SE 449 013
Opened 1876 and closed 1986 and now the site of Humphry Davy House, a nurses home. This view is dated 20th December 1986. [61437 Anonymous donation]

Manvers Main Colliery, Wath upon Dearne, South Yorkshire. SE 449 013
A view dated 20th December 1986. [61437 Anonymous donation]

Micklefield Colliery Explosion Memorial, St Mary's Churchyard, Great North Road, Micklefield, West Yorkshire. SE 445 328
The Monument erected to the memory of the 63 men who lost their lives on 30th April 1896 at Peckfield Colliery. Photographed 5th January 1993. [AA93/00969 Bob Skingle]

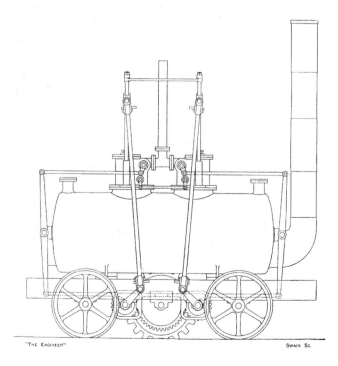

"THE ENGINEER"   SWAIN Sc.

Middleton Colliery Railway, Leeds, West Yorkshire.
In 1758 the first *Railway Act* was passed, authorising a rail or plate-way from Middleton to the centre of Leeds. In 1810, John Blenkinsop, manager of Middleton Colliery, engaged Matthew Murray to build a steam locomotive to run on this railway and on the 24th June 1812 the locomotive *Salamanca* became the first commercial steam train. The locomotive used the rack and pinion method of traction. Shown here is an illustration from *The Engineer* of 18th June 1920. "The boiler had a cast iron shell with a circular straight-through wrought iron flue and a wrought iron chimney. It was fixed to a timber carriage supported on four carrying wheels and was provided with a spring-loaded safety valve at each end. The two vertical cylinders were double-acting and were placed on top of the boiler, with more than half their length immersed in its steam space." (James Dunlop) [AA046220]

Mitchell Main Colliery, Wombwell, South Yorkshire. SE 392 041
A view dated March 1950. The colliery closed in 1956. [AA041986 Professor Stanley Beaver]

Mitchell Main Colliery, Wombwell, South Yorkshire. SE 392 041
Diversion of the river Dove, seen from a dirt stack. Photographed 12th August 1952. [BB95/09577]

Monckton Coke Works, Royston, Havercroft with Cold Hiendley, West Yorkshire. SE 375 122.
Also known as The Royston Works it was confusingly, the site of New Monckton Nos.1 and 2 Collieries.
The area is one of great complexity, with coal having been won locally from the 17th century. George Arundel-Monckton, Viscount Galway, of Hodroyd Hall, instigated large scale undertakings on his land leading to the establishment of a brickworks by 1875. Shortly afterwards coal mining and coke making eclipsed the brickworks and by the 1920s the coke ovens and by-product plant became the Monckton Coke and Chemical Company. The coke ovens shown here dated from a rebuild of 1976-9. The works is now a subsidiary within the UK Coal group and produces high quality metallurgical coke made from coal mined at Maltby colliery. A general view seen from the north. Photographed 19th January 1993. [AA93/00955 Bob Skingle]

Monckton Coke Works, Royston, Havercroft with Cold Hiendley, West Yorkshire. SE 375 122
A loaded coke car. Photographed 19th January 1993. [AA93/00936 Bob Skingle]

Monckton Coke Works, Royston, Havercroft with Cold Hiendley, West Yorkshire. SE 375 122
A view along the ovens with a coke car in position. Photographed 19th January 1993.
[AA93/00935 Bob Skingle]

127

Monckton Coke Works, Royston, Havercroft with Cold Hiendley, West Yorkshire. SE 375 122
A coke car being loaded as an oven is emptied. Photographed on 19th January 1993. [AA93/00933 Bob Skingle]

Monckton Coke Works, Royston, Havercroft with Cold Hiendley, West Yorkshire. SE 375 122
Cleaning an oven sill. Photographed 19th January 1993. [AA93/03707 James O Davies]

Monckton Coke Works, Royston, Havercroft with Cold Hiendley, West Yorkshire. SE 375 122
Cleaning an oven sill. Photographed 19th January 1993. [AA93/03701 James O Davies]

Monckton Coke Works, Royston, Havercroft with Cold Hiendley, West Yorkshire. SE 375 122
A view of the old winding gear house seen from the northeast. Photographed 19th January 1993.
[AA93/00953 Bob Skingle]

Monckton Coke Works, Royston, Havercroft with Cold Hiendley, West Yorkshire. SE 375 122
Carbonisation operators in front of the oven battery. Photographed 19th January 1993.
[AA93/03705 James O Davies]

Monckton Coke Works, Royston, Havercroft with Cold Hiendley, West Yorkshire. SE 375 122
Detail of old steam pumps. Photographed 19th January 1993. [AA93/00950 Bob Skingle]

Monckton Coke Works, Royston, Havercroft with Cold Hiendley, West Yorkshire. SE 375 122
Bernard Shaw, coke handling operator. Photographed 19th January 1993. [AA93/03704 James O Davies]

Moorends football stadium, Grange Road, Moorends, Thorne, South Yorkshire.
Grange Road was built 1920-30 in semi-detached blocks as part of a planned mining settlement. The stadium was built by the Miners Welfare Committee. Coal wagons are relatively uncommon survivals, two more can be seen in Peel Square, Barnsley, placed as a memorial in 1994. Photographed 6th April 1993. [AA93/01709 Roger Thomas]

Morley Main Colliery, Dewsbury, West Yorkshire.

From *The Illustrated London News*, 19th October 1872:

'The terrible disaster at the Morley Main Colliery, near Dewsbury, on Monday week, by which about forty men and boys lost their lives, was an explosion of the inflammable gas; and there is too much cause for believing that it was due to the carelessness of some of the men, in using lucifer-matches where they were working. At the adjourned inquest, on Saturday, evidence was given that in the pockets of the deceased, matches, fusees, tobacco, and pipes, and a key where-with to open the safety lamp, were found; and Ralph Berry, the underground steward, spoke to having smelled tobacco-smoke in the pit two hours before the explosion; but this did not strike him as being an out-of-the way occurrence. The inquest was again adjourned. The narratives of survivors and explorers describe the state of things in the mine during thirty-six hours after the explosion. When the first exploring party went down, led by Mr. William Ackroyd, jun., one of the partners, and Mr. James Simpkins, the principal steward, a shocking sight presented itself. The dead and dying were lying about on every side, and the groans of the injured were heartrending. Here and there were the carcasses of some of the small horses used in the "gigs" or tramways for drawing corves. Eleven of these animals were killed. Corves filled with coal were overturned by the force of the explosion. One of the dead men had an empty matchbox in his hand when he was picked up. The dead were found in various positions, but most of them had apparently fallen on their faces to escape from the suffocating gas, called "after-damp" which at last overcame them. The bratticing and other means of ventilation were completely destroyed, and much labour was entailed in providing temporary means of ventilation. The colliery was reopened for working on Monday last.' [BB016194]

Miner's Institute, Barnsley Road, Moorthorpe, South Elmsall, West Yorkshire. SE 463 111
A view taken from the northeast, 5th January 1993. [AA93/00973 Bob Skingle]

Miner's Institute, Barnsley Road, Moorthorpe. South Elmsall, West Yorkshire. SE 463 111
Detail of miner at work, carved in the pediment. Photographed 5th January 1993. [AA93/00971 Bob Skingle]

New Crofton Estate, Crofton, West Yorkshire. SE 387 174
Early 20th century miners' housing in seven streets, with allotment gardens to the west. Remarkably there appeared to be no Institute, Mission Hall or shop. Here we see the northwest end including the Chapel, looking down Third Street, 6th December 1982.
[BB83/02384 Bob Skingle]

Right: New Crofton Estate, Crofton, West Yorkshire. SE 387 174
Fourth Street. Photographed 6th December 1982.
[YO 717 Peter Williams]

Below: New Crofton Estate, Crofton, West Yorkshire. SE 387 174
Sixth Street. Photographed 6th December 1982.
[BB83/02396 Bob Skingle]

North Gawber Colliery, Gawber, Barnsley, South Yorkshire. SK 331 098
Sunk 1869 and closed in 1987. This view was taken on the 27th February 1988. [61439 Anonymous donation.]

North Gawber Colliery, Gawber, Barnsley, South Yorkshire. SK 331 098
The Non-condensing Bull steam engine of 1852, used as a mine pump, photographed in 1950 by George Watkins. The cast iron plate reads "T.N.G.B.I.C.S. Gazette Extraordinary 1852" [SER 359 Watkins Collection, NMR]

National Union of Mine Workers' Offices, Victoria Road, Barnsley, South Yorkshire.
SE 343 070
A grade II listed building, built 1874, by Wade and Turner, as the headquarters of the South Yorkshire and North Derbyshire Miners' Union. Outside the front of the building stands the Memorial to the Yorkshire Miners' Association – notably commemorating John Normansell who was General Secretary from 1864 to 1875.
[AA92/07018 Bob Skingle]

National Union of Mineworkers' Offices, Victoria Road, Barnsley, South Yorkshire.
SE 343 070
An interior view of the main lecture hall, taken 20th January 1993. Hanging on the wall to the left can be seen the marching banner of the Wombwell Main Branch.
[AA93/02660 James O Davies]

National Union of Mineworkers' Offices, Victoria Road, Barnsley, South Yorkshire. SE 343 070
A stained glass roundel depicting a miner wearing rescue apparatus. [AA93/02663 James O Davies]

National Union of Mineworkers' Offices, Victoria Road, Barnsley, South Yorkshire. SE 343 070
A stained glass roundel depicting a collier at the coal face. [AA93/03445 James O Davies]

National Union of Mineworkers' Offices, Victoria Road, Barnsley, South Yorkshire. SE 343 070
A stained glass roundel showing a collier pushing a tub of coal. [AA 93/003447 James O Davies]

National Union of Mineworkers' Offices, Victoria Road, Barnsley, South Yorkshire. SE 343 070
A stained glass roundel depicting a pit pony at work. [AA93/03446 James O Davies]

National Union of Mineworkers' Offices, Victoria Road, Barnsley, South Yorkshire. SE 343 070
A stained glass roundel depicting colliers descending in a cage. [AA93/03450 James O Davies]

National Union of Mineworkers' Offices, Victoria Road, Barnsley, South Yorkshire. SE 343 070
A stained glass roundel depicting two colliers with a tub of coal at pithead. [AA93/03448 James O Davies]

National Union of Mineworkers' Offices, Victoria Road, Barnsley, South Yorkshire. SE 343 070
A stained glass roundel depicting a coal tippler. [AA93/03451 James O Davies]

National Union of Mineworkers' Offices, Victoria Road, Barnsley, South Yorkshire. SE 343 070
A stained glass roundel depicting a safety lamp and tools. [AA93/02664 James O Davies]

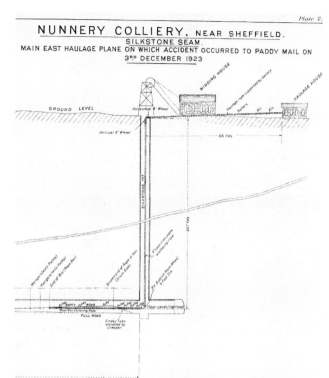

NUNNERY COLLIERY, NEAR SHEFFIELD.
SILKSTONE SEAM.
MAIN EAST HAULAGE PLANE ON WHICH ACCIDENT OCCURRED TO PADDY MAIL ON
3RD DECEMBER 1923

Nunnery Colliery, Sheffield, South Yorkshire.
A plan from the *Report on the Causes of and Circumstances attending the Underground Haulage Accident which occurred at the Nunnery Colliery, near Sheffield, on the 3rd December 1923* by Sir Thomas H Mottram, C.B.E. Seven persons lost their lives and 55 others were injured when the steel haulage rope broke whilst 120 miners descended the main haulage plane in the 'paddy mail'. [BB016210]

Nunnery Colliery, Sheffield, South Yorkshire.
The site of the accident. [BB016211]

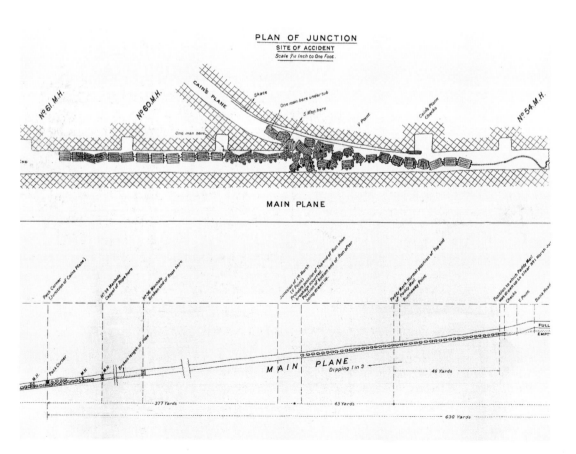

PLAN OF JUNCTION
SITE OF ACCIDENT
Scale ½ Inch to One Foot.

MAIN PLANE

THE GREAT ARDSLEY MAIN COLLIERY.

The Oaks Colliery or The Great Ardsley Main Colliery, Barnsley, South Yorkshire.
In July 1845 an explosion of fire damp had killed three miners and in December 1845 there was a fire in the pit. In March 1847 another dreadful explosion of fire damp resulted in the loss of 73 lives. *The Illustrated London News*, 13th March 1847. [BB016203]

THE FUNERAL.

The Oaks Colliery or The Great Ardsley Main Colliery, Barnsley, South Yorkshire.
A view of the funeral, from *The Illustrated London News* 13th March 1847.
"This disaster has cast around the town of Barnsley and neighbourhood a deeper gloom than has ever been experienced. It embraces, indeed, by far the greatest sacrifice of life than has ever occurred in that locality. We believe in no colliery explosion in Yorkshire has there ever been so great a loss as at Barnsley. The afternoon of Monday presented as melancholy a picture as the eye could witness – nearly fifty of the sufferers being interred at the parish church and the funeral procession at one time extended more than half a mile in length. The shops of the tradesmen were closed, and the bells rang dumb peals." [BB016204]

THE SECOND EXPLOSION AT THE OAKS COLLIERY, BARNSLEY.—SEE PRECEDING PAGE.

The Oaks Colliery or The Great Ardsley Main Colliery, Barnsley, South Yorkshire.
The worst mining disaster in England occurred on 12th December 1866 when two explosions took the lives of 361 miners. This view from *The Illustrated London News* 22nd December 1866 shows the cage thrown up into the headgear. [BB016196]

The Oaks Colliery or The Great Ardsley Main Colliery, Barnsley, South Yorkshire.
Another view from *The Illustrated London News* 22nd December 1866, showing the scene after the second explosion. [BB016195]

The Oaks Colliery or The Great Ardsley Main Colliery, Barnsley, South Yorkshire.
A general view from *The Illustrated London News* 29th December 1866. [BB016198]

The Oaks Colliery or The Great Ardsley Main Colliery, Barnsley, South Yorkshire.
Filling the cupola shaft to stop the draught of air. *The Illustrated London News* 29th December 1866. [BB016197]

The Oaks Colliery Explosion Memorial, Doncaster Road, Kendray, Barnsley, South Yorkshire. SE 352 058
Erected 1913 by Wade and Turner with stonework by Dalby and iron railings by C Downing. Photographed 19th November 1992. [AA92/07015 Bob Skingle]

Orgreave Colliery, Orgreave, South Yorkshire. SK 424 871
A general view of the headframe and winding house. Photographed 14th November 1976. [26/23 George Cooper]

Orgreave Colliery, Orgreave, South Yorkshire. SK 424 871
A general view including the chimney. Photographed 14th November 1976. [26/24 George Cooper]

Orgreave Colliery, Orgreave, South Yorkshire. SK 424 871
A general view of the No.1 winding engine house. Photographed 14th November 1976. [26/21 George Cooper]

Orgreave Colliery, Orgreave, South Yorkshire. SK 424 871
A view of the horizontal duplex winder by Markham and Company Ltd, Chesterfield, 1926. Photographed 14th November 1976. [26/04 George Cooper]

Orgreave Colliery, Orgreave, South Yorkshire. SK 424 871
A view of the horizontal duplex winder, taken on the 14th November 1976. [26/11 George Cooper]

Premier Lamp and Engineering Company, Leeds, West Yorkshire.
A carbide cap lamp c1930. The reaction between water and calcium carbide produces acetylene gas. [AA049279 Peter Williams]

Prince of Wales Colliery, Park Road, Pontefract, West Yorkshire. SE 4506 2284
Established in 1869 by John Rhodes Colliery Company, subsequently purchased by Glass Houghton Colliery Company in 1928 and modernised. Extensively rebuilt in the 1970s, the 'Ponty Prince' closed in 2003. A general view from the southeast, taken 4th June 1993. [AA93/03846 Roger Thomas]

Prince of Wales Colliery, Park Road, Pontefract, West Yorkshire. SE 4506 2284
A view of the intake drift portal. Photographed 4th June 1993. [AA93/03842 Roger Thomas]

Prince of Wales Colliery, Park Road, Pontefract, West Yorkshire. SE 4506 2284
No.1 winding engine house from the south. Photographed 4th June 1993. [AA93/03824 Roger Thomas]

Prince of Wales Colliery, Park Road, Pontefract, West Yorkshire. SE 4506 2284
A general view from the south. Photographed 4th June 1993. [AA93/03827 Roger Thomas]

Prince of Wales Colliery, Park Road, Pontefract, West Yorkshire. SE 4506 2284
The breaker house viewed from the east. Photographed 4th June 1993. [AA93/03834 Roger Thomas]

Prince of Wales Colliery, Park Road, Pontefract, West Yorkshire. SE 4506 2284
The rapid loading bunker viewed from the south. Photographed 4th June 1993. [AA93/03831 Roger Thomas]

Prince of Wales Colliery, Park Road, Pontefract, West Yorkshire. SE 4506 2284
A view of the stockyard from the east. Photographed 4th June 1993. [AA93/03851 Roger Thomas]

Prince of Wales Colliery, Park Road, Pontefract, West Yorkshire. SE 4506 2284
The canteen. Photographed 4th June 1993. [AA93/03840 Roger Thomas]

Prince of Wales Colliery, Park Road, Pontefract, West Yorkshire. SE 4506 2284
The boot-wash. Photographed 4th June 1993. [AA93/03809 Roger Thomas]

Redbrook Colliery, Gawber, Barnsley, South Yorkshire. SE 328 079
Remarkable for its underground Christmas carol services c1949-1960, the colliery closed in 1987. Shown here is the older headframe and winding house. Photographed 27th February, 1988. [61438 Anonymous donation]

Redbrook Colliery, Gawber, Barnsley, South Yorkshire. SE 328 079
A view of the modernist 1970s headframe and offices. Photographed 27th February 1988. [61438 Anonymous donation]

Rossington Colliery, West End Lane, New Rossington, South Yorkshire. SK 6012 9833
Sinking commenced at No.2 Shaft on the 26th June 1912 and the Barnsley seam reached on the 7th November 1915 at 872 yards. The headgear and heapstead to No.2 Shaft viewed from the northeast, 10th May 1993. The structure was built in two phases, the first phase of c1915 was later enclosed by the taller open framed steel frame seen here. Unusually there are no backlegs. [AA93/03113 Keith Buck]

Rossington Colliery, West End Lane, New Rossington, South Yorkshire. SK 6012 9833
No.2 Shaft, electric winder house and heapstead viewed from the southwest. Photographed 10th May 1993.
[AA93/03123 Keith Buck]

Rossington Colliery, West End Lane, New Rossington, South Yorkshire. SK 6012 9833
The No.1 winding engine house, dating to 1915 but superseded by a new electric winder house c1960, here seen used as a power house. Photographed 10th May 1993. [AA93/03117 Keith Buck]

Rossington Colliery, West End Lane, New Rossington, South Yorkshire. SK 6012 9833
The stores range dating to 1912-20 viewed from the north. Photographed 10th May 1993. [AA93/03124 Keith Buck]

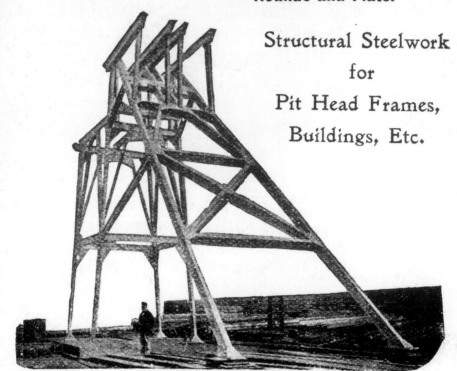

WALTER SCOTT
LIMITED

Leeds.   LEEDS STEEL WORKS.   England.

MANUFACTURERS OF . . .
ROLLED STEEL JOISTS, CHANNELS, Etc.,
Mild Steel Blooms, Billets, Slabs, Tinbars.
Rounds and Flats.

Structural Steelwork
for
Pit Head Frames,
Buildings, Etc.

BRITISH STANDARD TRAMRAILS, AND
PERMANENT WAY RAILS.

Books of Sections and other information on application.

Walter Scott Limited, Leeds Steel Works, Leeds, West Yorkshire.
An advertisement from *The Colliery Managers Pocket Book* 1918. [BB016217]

Selby Project, Gascoigne Wood Drift, South Milford, North Yorkshire. SE 523 318
An aerial view, taken 19th October 1992, showing the enormous scale of operations. At the time the 'Selby Superpit' was said to be the largest coal mining venture in the world. In 1993-4 12 million tonnes of coal were raised. Geological faults have been blamed for the abandonment of massive underground reserves and the complex closed in October 2004. Two massive drifts at top of picture disgorge coal to the holding area in the foreground and rapid loading bunkers sit atop the railway line to the upper right. [CCX 14364/11 Cox Collection, NMR]

Selby Project, Whitemoor Mine, Cliffe, North Yorkshire. SE 665 356
One of the five satellite shaft mines serving Gascoigne Wood, seen here 19th October 1992.
[CCX 14360/11 Cox Collection, NMR]

Selby Project, Whitemoor Mine, Cliffe, North Yorkshire. SE 665 356
An aerial view. Photographed 29th June 1999. [NMR 17282/07]

Sharlston Colliery, Sharlston, West Yorkshire. SE 361 180
The Colliery Band. Photographed 20th January 1993. [AA93/03715 James O Davies]

Sharlston Colliery Miners Welfare, Sharlston, West Yorkshire.
Playing pool. Photographed 26th January 1993. [AA93/03710 James O Davies]

Shuttle Eye Colliery, Grange Moor, Kirkburton, West Yorkshire. SE 222 156
A plaque on the cement capping to No.2 Shaft gives the infill date as 24th November 1992. The horizontal duplex steam winder by Bradley and Craven, Wakefield, 1930 is seen here in a ruinous condition. Photographed 12th September 1976. [08/2-18 George Cooper]

Shuttle Eye Colliery, Grange Moor, Kirkburton, West Yorkshire. SE 222 156
Another view of the steam winder. Photographed 12th September 1976. [08/2-18 George Cooper]

Silverwood Colliery, Rotherham, South Yorkshire. SK 477 939
A general view including the east and west winders and the engineers shop from the east. Photographed 12th November 1991. [BB91/23495 Bob Skingle]

Silverwood Colliery, Rotherham, South Yorkshire. SK 477 939
A view of the lamp room office. Photographed 12th November 1991. [BB91/23480 Bob Skingle]

Swaithe Main Colliery, Worsbrough, South Yorkshire.
On 6th December 1875 an explosion of firedamp ignited by shot firing resulted in 143 deaths. At this time, the fund of £48,000 raised after The Oaks Colliery explosion of 1866, stood at £34,000 in hand, with widows receiving 6 shillings per week. Whereas the provision of basic relief seems to have been socially acceptable, a final dispersal of the fund to widows and orphans by way of compensation would have raised them up above their station and concerns were expressed by the press that further fund raising for the Swaithe Main disaster would be unacceptable. A view of the colliery from *The Illustrated London News*, 18th December 1875. [BB016207]

Swaithe Main Colliery, Worsbrough, South Yorkshire.
An underground scene 'Finding the dead bodies'. *The Illustrated London News*, 18th December 1875. [BB016208]

Swaithe Main Colliery Explosion Memorial, Church of St Thomas and St James, Bank End Road, Worsbrough, South Yorkshire. SE 351 030
Photographed 8th January 1993.
[AA93/01087 Bob Skingle]

Swaithe Main Colliery Explosion Memorial, Church of St Thomas and St James, Bank End Road, Worsbrough, South Yorkshire. SE 351 030
A roundel showing a mining scene.
Photographed 8th January 1993.
[AA93/ 01089 Bob Skingle]

Tankersley Rescue Station, Tankersley, South Yorkshire. SK 346 006
This was the first mines rescue station in England, built 1902. On the 21st July 1908 the Superintendent of Tankersley Rescue Station, Walter Clifford, received the Edward VII 1st Class Medal (the Miners' Victoria Cross) for bravery at the Hamstead Colliery fire. Photographed 27th January, 1993.
[AA93/01458 Bob Skingle]

THE ILLUSTRATED LONDON NEWS

THE COLLIERY RIOTS IN YORKSHIRE.

Tankersley Colliery Riots.
Escorting the prisoners to the courthouse at Barnsley in 1870. A dispute between striking unionist colliers and owners, Newton Chambers and Company, had led to an attack upon the strike breakers at Westwood Row. Arrests were made, and when the 28 prisoners were first brought before the Barnsley Magistrates, a 'tumult in the streets' raised fears of mob rule. Three companies of the 22nd Regiment and a squadron of the 13th Hussars plus 160 members of the West Yorkshire Constabulary conducted the prisoners from Wakefield Gaol back to Barnsley for the inquiry. Twenty three men were subsequently sent to trial at the Assize Court. *The Illustrated London News* for 19th February 1870.   [BB016193]

Thurnscoe Miners Housing, Thurnscoe, Dearne, South Yorkshire. SE 464 054
Derelict housing. Photographed 10th November 1993. [AA94/00345 Bob Skingle]

Tom Pudding Barges, Aire and Calder Navigation, Castleford, West Yorkshire. SE 425 260
Seen here at a lock on the Aire and Calder canal is a train of compartment boats, or pans, being pushed by a Bantum tug. Used by Cawoods Hargreaves to ferry coal from Kellingley Colliery, these compartment boats are the descendants of the original barges developed by W H Bartholomew in the 1860s to take coal to Goole dock. The barges were lifted by hydraulic hoists and the contents tipped into seagoing colliers. The original Tom Puddings would have had a jebus or false bow – unlike the boat shown. Photographed 8th January 1993.
[AA93/01050 Bob Skingle]

Tom Pudding Barges, Aire and Calder Navigation, Castleford, West Yorkshire. SE 425 260
Another view of the train of compartment boats. Photographed 8th January 1993.
[AA93/01051 Bob Skingle]

Treeton Colliery, Well Lane, Treeton, South Yorkshire. SK 432 876
Sunk 1875-6 by Rothervale Collieries Ltd, production ended 7th December 1990.
A view of the entrance, taken 14th December 1990. [202F-27]

Treeton Colliery, Well Lane, Treeton, South Yorkshire. SK 432 876
A view taken 14th December 1990. [202D – 24]

Treeton Colliery, Well Lane, Treeton, South Yorkshire. SK 432 876
A view of the General Offices with the old sheave wheels in the foreground, taken 14th December 1990.
[202F – 21]

Treeton Colliery, Well Lane, Treeton, South Yorkshire. SK 432 876
A view of Front Street and a hint of Pit Lane. It is thought that Treeton was the first colliery village to have electric
street lighting. Photographed 14th December 1990. [202F – 31]

Above: Waleswood Colliery, Mansfield Road, Wales, South Yorkshire. SK 45 83
Dating from the late 19th century, closure came in May 1948. The engine house was subsequently used as a training facility for winding enginemen, whilst No.1 shaft continued as a pumping station for Kiveton Park. A view from the west. Photographed 7th May 1993. [AA94/00321 Keith Buck]

Above: Waleswood Colliery, Mansfield Road, Wales, South Yorkshire. SK 45 83
Winding engine instrumentation.
Photographed 7th May 1993.
[AA94/00319 Keith Buck]

Waleswood Colliery, Mansfield Road, Wales, South Yorkshire. SK 4671 8383
The winding engine was originally built by Worsley Mesnes Ironworks Ltd., Wigan. The engine and drum shown sits upon the cast iron bed of the original.
[AA94/0320 Keith Buck]

Walton Colliery, Walton, West Yorkshire. SE 360 182
The 'new shaft' at Walton was sunk in 1890 and the mine developed rapidly with its good rail connections. Coal production ended on the 3rd December 1979 and the site is now a 72 hectare nature park. Unfortunately it was not possible for a significant part of the building or headframe to be preserved as a monument. The east end of the power house with boilers in the foreground, taken 15th June 1981. [BB81/ 03548 Peter Williams]

Walton Colliery, Walton, West Yorkshire. SE 360 182
Headstocks to No.1 and No.2 Shafts from the southwest during demolition. Photographed 15 June 1981.
[BB81/03549 Terry Buchanan]

Walton Colliery, Walton, West Yorkshire. SE 360 182
The interior of the power house. Photographed 15th June 1981. [BB81/03569 Peter Williams]

Walton Colliery, Walton, West Yorkshire. SE 360 182
The No.2 winding house south engine. Photographed 15th June 1981. [BB81/03574 Peter Williams]

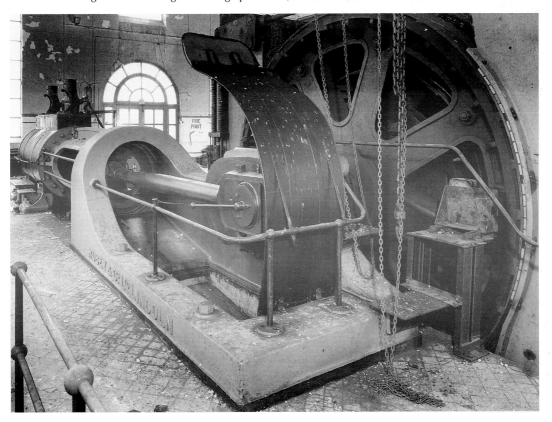

Walton Colliery, Walton, West Yorkshire. SE 360 182
The No.2 winding house north engine. Photographed 15th June 1981. [BB81/03571 Peter Williams]

Walton, West Yorkshire. SE 360 182
The tiled passage from No.3 winding house leading to the power house. Photographed 15th June 1981.
[BB81/03578 Peter Williams]

Wath Colliery, Wath upon Dearne, South Yorkshire. SE 435 019
Sunk in 1873, this view was taken 20th December 1986, just prior to demolition.
[61436 Anonymous donation]

Wath Colliery, Wath upon Dearne, South Yorkshire. SE 435 019
A general view taken 20th December 1986. [61436 Anonymous donation]

Wharncliffe Carlton Colliery, Barnsley, South Yorkshire.
A disastrous explosion caused the loss of 20 lives on the 18ᵗʰ October 1883. *The Illustrated London News* 3rd November 1883. [BB016199]

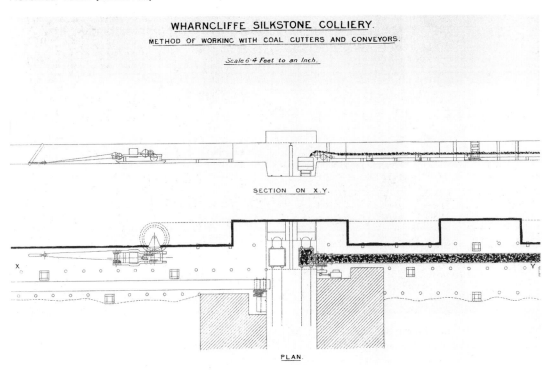

Wharncliffe Silkstone Colliery, Barnsley, South Yorkshire.
Dating from 1853, the colliery was closed in 1966. A copy of a plan showing the method of working coal cutters and conveyors taken from the Report on the circumstances attending an explosion on 30ᵗʰ May 1914. [BB01612]

Wharncliffe Silkstone Colliery, Barnsley, South Yorkshire.
The single cylinder vertical non-condensing steam winding engine, made by A&G Davies, Tipton, Staffordshire, 1855. Photographed in 1954. [SER 626 Watkins Collection, NMR]

The Wheldale Public House, Wheldon Road, Castleford, West Yorkshire. SE 436 261
Pub sign. Henry Moore, son of a Castleford coal-miner, visited the Wheldale Colliery in 1941-2 and made some
evocative drawings of the miners at work. Photographed 11th January 1993. [AA93/1005 Bob Skingle]

Whitby Jet.
Whatever the geological argument may be as to the origin and classification of jet, in the popular imagination it is considered to be a type of coal, formed from the remains of the araucaria tree. Should you desire to set fire to your jet jewellery, it will burn with the smell of a coal fire. It is found in the bituminous shales between Robin Hoods Bay and Boulby. The jet industry reached its peak c1870 when 200 miners, or 'jetties' supplied 1,500 production workers. Jet production followed the fashion for 'mourning jewellery' popularised by Queen Victoria. Roman jet ornaments from the Yorkshire Archaeological Museum, photographed in 1960. [RY349]

Whitby Jet.
Three late 19th century jet brooches. [DP00511 Ian Savage]

Whitby Jet.
A jet chess piece dating to the 12th century excavated at Whitby Abbey hard garden in 2001. The white metal inlay is a tin/lead mix. [AA036175 Ian Leonard]

Cottage, Sowood Lane, Whitley Lower, Kirkburton, West Yorkshire. SE 227 164
An abandoned single-stored colliers cottage, photographed 15th January 1993. Behind it lay a spoil heap marked as 'Old Coal Pit' on the 1850 OS map. [AA93/01383 Bob Skingle]

Whitwood Terrace and Institute, Whitwood Common Lane, Castleford, West Yorkshire. SE 404 242
Whitwood Colliery was sunk in 1874 and closed c1970. The owners, Henry Briggs Son and Co Ltd engaged CFA Voysey to design new housing. Seen here is a watercolour perspective of the Institute and Terrace by CFA Voysey 1904. [BB83/03724 ©RIBA]

Whitwood Terrace and Institute, Whitwood Common Lane, Castleford, West Yorkshire. SE 404 242
The Terrace and Rising Sun Public House. Photographed 18th February 1983. [YO738 Peter Williams]

The Wolf Safety Lamp Co Ltd, Saxon Road Works, Sheffield, South Yorkshire.
Established by a German company in Leeds in the 1880s, ownership changed in 1913 and the business moved to Sheffield, finally arriving at Saxon Works in 1934. The inscription on the lamp shown reads; The Wolf Safety Lamp Co. (Wm Maurice) Ltd, Sheffield. Type FS. [BB016223 Peter Williams]

Woodlands Colliery Village, Adwick-le-Street, South Yorkshire. SE 53 07
In 1906 Sir Arthur Markham planned a great expansion at Brodsworth Main Colliery and determined to house the workforce in a 'garden city' community village. Percy Houfton was engaged as architect and he applied an Arts and Crafts style to the estate. A view of Green lane, 13th February 1989. [BB94/14756 Bob Skingle]

Yorkshire Main Colliery, Edlington, South Yorkshire. SK 544 992
A view of the Markham horizontal duplex winder of 1909. Photographed 28th April 1979.
[79/10/6A George Cooper]

Yorkshire Main Colliery, Edlington, South Yorkshire. SK 544 992
Another view of the Markham horizontal duplex winder of 1909. [79/10/36 George Cooper]

Yorkshire Colliers.
Colliery strikes took place in South Yorkshire, Derbyshire and Nottinghamshire in 1893, when the colliery owners tried to reduce wages by 25%. A bitter struggle resulted between the newly formed Miners' Federation of Great Britain and the owners, and in South Yorkshire 253 pits were closed and 80,971 men were made idle. On the 7th September 1893, at Ackton Hall Colliery, protesting miners were fired on by troops. Sixteen men were wounded and two killed in the infamous 'Featherstone Massacre'. Public sympathy was with the striking miners and their families. After sixteen weeks the strike ended with the men returning to work at the old rates. The 'great lock out' was instrumental in paving the way for Union bargaining, arbitration and the eight-hour day. The sketch shows four miners who could be seen today in any Yorkshire mining town or village. *The Illustrated London News* 16th September 1893. [BB016200]

Index